THE

SNARLING

CITIZEN

Barbara Ehrenreich

THE

SNARLING

CITIZEN

E S S A Y S

Farrar, Straus and Giroux

New York

To my aunt Jean,

the funniest woman on earth

Contents

THE

SNARLING

CITIZEN

Introduction

In the old days journalists vied for the zeitgeist watch. To be assigned to the zeitgeist meant that you could be trusted with an expense account and allowed out of the office during work hours. Veteran geist-watchers used the money to finance a cab ride to some arbitrary destination, interviewed the cab driver, and had their story written by late afternoon. Today, however, journalists fear to leave their desks lest their health insurance be canceled while they are out, and few cabbies can communicate outside their native Russian or Arabic. Geist-watching has sedimented to the lowest ranks of the journalism profession—freelancers, like myself; guest essayists; and illegal immigrants who lack the skills that are required in the restaurant industry.

The problem is that zeitgeist-watching is no longer considered an outdoor activity, worthy of Pulitzers and five-figure pay. Every home now has geist-gauging equipment, generally located in the bedrooms and den, and even children are capable of turning it on and operating it by remote. Hence the expectation that geist-watchers and social commentators will generally pursue their professions while performing some other small but remunerative task, such as babysitting for the neighbors' children or knitting ski caps for sale.

This is, in fact, how most of the insights in the following essays were obtained. First comes the phone call or, most likely, just a message on the answering machine from the editor of one of our major media outlets. "Barbara," the voice says, or at least some similar-sounding name, "I hope I have the right number because we need the Mood in America (or the Future of Life on Earth, or Whatever Happened to Our Way of Life?) by Thursday at the latest. And if I've got the wrong number, I'd appreciate knowing if there's someone else there who could do it instead." Then, flattered and brimming with investigative zeal, I rush to the den, wrestle the remote out of a loved one's hand, and settle down to work.

It's not as easy as you may be imagining, this geist-gazing, insight-garnering line of work. There are the difficulties attendant on any form of home work, as opposed to that performed in factories or offices. Children screaming underfoot, for example, when you happen to step on them or remark that most other twenty-two-year-olds are out in the workforce by now. Neighbors fleeing homicidal family members, oily-toned telemarketers arriving by phone, elderly dependents who must be shooed away from the six-pack in the fridge lest they exhaust their supply of Attends.

But I persist, hour after hour, clicking doggedly away at the remote. Sometimes days go by with no palpable product, only a swirl of numbing patter enlivened by jokes about body functions and tips on the cleaning of dentures. The neighbors admire my attention span, the ability to remain glued to my work no matter how painful or exhausting. The take-out containers mount up; phone calls go unanswered; pets sicken and die; family members pack up and move to distant states, leaving only their house keys behind.

Then, sometimes when you least expect it, the zeitgeist

begins to emerge from the screen. If you were hoping maybe for a winged and helmeted figure of noble visage, then you have been reading too much Hegel and not watching enough CNN. Our contemporary zeitgeist is a low, snarly creature that oozes out from the TV and settles lumplike in the middle of the den, where it pulses lethargically and makes an occasional lunge for the dog. And here is another reason why well-paid celebrity journalists will have nothing to do with the zeitgeist anymore: it is not the kind of thing you would like to find on your family-room floor.

The modern zeitgeist feeds on images, though historians tell us that in the distant past it ate rougher stuff, like raw experience and epic poems. Now it wants images night and day, and it hardly matters to the zeitgeist whether the scenes it consumes are the result of actual real-world events or artful cinematic deception. The bloated corpses on the screen may be the product of painful human deaths or of extras working for hourly wages. They can be the victims of genocidal clashes in Bosnia or Rwanda, of some deranged celebrity killer in Brentwood, California, or of Arnold Schwarzenegger on a fictional rampage—the zeitgeist finds them almost equally tasty.

There are times, I will admit, when the zeitgeist can be an amusing companion and a refreshing break from the so-called real world of traffic jams, collection agencies, and malls. When it's been snacking on a delicious presidential sex scandal, for example, or an outbreak of mayhem on the Olympic figure-skating team—at such moments the whole family troops merrily into the den, nachos and bean dip in hand. For who cannot be charmed by the zeitgeist as it pounces playfully on some topic or personality, chews it to shreds, and then rolls over, sated, to wait for the next?

But, as we know all too well, it can turn nasty overnight. After feeding long enough on stories of crime and the transgressions of foreign rulers, or when it has been whipped into a frenzy by foam-mouthed right-wing preachers and talk-show hosts, the zeitgeist can assume a form that is menacing to human life. It swells until it fills the entire room and spills out onto the lawn, screaming with infantile rage, clawing at the sky, howling for blood.

At such moments it is wise to remain huddled together indoors, preferably under the bed. When the geist craves blood, no one is entirely safe. Wars are declared, often against populations that have no clear idea what transgressions their rulers may have committed. New prisons are slapped together, young people are paddled and caned. Human sacrifices may even be required, preferably of criminals who have exhausted their right to appeal. For the zeitgeist, fully aroused, resembles nothing so much as a toddler in a tantrum or a full-grown Republican in a characteristic outbreak of punitive rage.

It was not supposed to be this way, of course. Important pundits and dreamers had announced that the zeitgeist of the 1990s would be distinctively different from its 1980s incarnation. Greed and violence would give way to "acts of random kindness and senseless beauty"; the military would wither away, leaving a lavish peace dividend in its place; "government" would come to mean something other than the IRS. And for ten seconds of historical time, it almost looked as if these predictions would come true. We put a cuddly new president in the White House, a man with a feisty wife and mistresses and an unshakable commitment to a program defined boldly by the content-free word *change*. There was even some wild talk about a return of sex (long banned as a source of disease and offense to the Christian right), of domestic spending, of dancing in the street.

Within months though, the new president had himself been mauled by the geist. Oh, he did everything possible to appease it, with the help of his able wife. No president had ever studied it so carefully, monitored it with so many polls, and attempted so earnestly to charm it with smiles and beguile it with charts and graphs. He darted to the right, and then to the right, and yet again further to the right. The Haitians were abandoned for years to tread water with the sharks; the Iraqis were bombed and rebombed; workers continued to be mocked with an hourly minimum wage that barely exceeds a skycap's tip; little kids on welfare were threatened with starvation if their mothers didn't go out and cook burgers for strangers. Yet somehow the zeitgeist was not appeased, and began instead to see in Bill Clinton a cruel caricature of its own unloveliest traits—fickleness, mendacity, and a craving for high-fat foods. The ferocity with which it turned on our poor head of state was terrible to watch.

No one had expected the zeitgeist to evolve into a living thing, capable of destroying grown men. It was supposed to be a mere emanation, a kind of mist rising from the general mind. But something happened, probably in the mid-1980s, that still baffles the psychosociological experts. Perhaps we had to reach some critical mass in terms of the number of people watching TV at any one time. This may have occurred when the airports installed CNN, or perhaps at the point when college students abandoned their books for *Melrose Place*. Then, for the first time in human history, hundreds of millions of individual minds were wired together in a single teleneurological system, inhabiting a self-contained universe of image and jingle and slogan.

Still, the zeitgeist might not have sprung to life if it had not been for the media's increasing reliance on ratings and polls. With these new computerized, high-tech mood-gauging instruments, the media folk can instantly tell how an image or idea is faring in the collective mind, and withdraw or reinforce that image at will, as required to keep the viewers transfixed. Thus the wiring that connects us all together goes not simply from "real world" to media to human mind but in the other direction as well. If you don't like "the news," if it drags or annoys, you can be sure it will be replaced soon by something better. Infotainment flows in one direction, polls and ratings in the other, to produce a simulated macrobrain. What has emerged, in layperson's terms, is a closed loop in which bizarre feedback phenomena readily develop, along with something eerily resembling biological life.

Who could have imagined such an outcome? Telecommunications, combined with computers and polls, were supposed to make us smarter, more connected, better able to right wrongs as we found them. But the collective mind that emerges from our vast media circuitry turns out to be cruder and more credulous than the sum of its parts. Individually we may hate injustice and love logic and reason. Wired together and resonating with infotainment, we become something terrifyingly different—a franken-geist.

Hence the hasty decline of what was once proudly known as the "political process." Not so long ago, the person seeking "change" of some sort, as our president terms it—the abolition of slavery, for example, or the preservation of one of our few remaining freestanding trees—would go from door to door, engaging the neighbors in earnest discussion. Arguments would be waged, pots of coffee consumed, doors slammed or petitions signed. The "process" would inch along. But today, that same change-oriented person would be an object of suspicion just for appearing out of doors and on foot. He or she would be labeled an "activist," a term suggesting some unfortunate tendency to fidget and twitch. And if a door ever opened to him or her, it would reveal a room full of citizens deeply engrossed in the plight of some homicidal car-rental spokesman or penisless former Marine. Slavery and trees would have to wait.

And what if our activist succeeded in calling attention to

some awful injustice or omen of environmental doom? Suppose people even began to picket and protest. Would the zeitgeist pay any attention—or would these small signs of human initiative be swallowed up in the onrush of unrelated imagery, self-righteous talk-show talk, new and improved products, celebrity trials, cop shows, and televised psychics?

So you can see there are hazards to this line of work. Perhaps no one can monitor the zeitgeist without being drawn ineluctably into it. After hours at my work, a certain fretfulness sets in, a sense of emptiness and total futility that can be relieved only by ever more vivid images and sensations—bigger and better wars, crimes involving torture and cannibalism!

At such times I am grateful for the small distractions that are part of a home worker's life. A sweet-faced child enters the den, clambers onto my shoulder or knee, and asks why we always have to have this gross-looking zeitgeist prowling around on the floor. Then, although the child is well into his or her twenties and is in danger of crushing my shoulder or knee, I am reminded that there are precious aspects of existence that cannot be accessed by clicking a remote.

It comes to me, in a surge of revolutionary insight, that our lives—meaning whatever it is that continues to happen when the TV is off and even when the power has failed—are richer and vastly more curious than anything we will find in the flickering realm of image and spectacle. That even those of us who will never be subjects for docudramas, who will never invent ingenious new ways of killing our family members and getting rid of the bodies—yes, even we who can never hope to enter the realm of image but who remain day after day in the nonvirtual world of tactile sensation—we also matter. We are, or are entitled to be, the heroes of at least our own lives. And that may be the most empowering and subversive insight available in this premillennial, postmodern era.

Act on it.

LIFE

IN THE

POSTMODERN

FAMILY

Burt, Loni, and

Our Way of Life

With Burt and Loni a thing of the past, we might as well kiss the institution of marriage goodbye. There they were, the very icons of middle-aged cuteness. And here they are now— sounding like one of the nastier mismatches from *The Love Connection*. Nor are they alone. Despite countless warnings about how divorce is destroying the very foundations of Western Civ, the U.S. divorce rate remains stuck near 50 percent, higher than that of any other country that bothers to keep track. Richard and Cindy are throwing in the towel, as may Michael and Lisa Marie.

"Permissiveness" is the standard explanation, meaning that we have become a slack-willed race, slaves to every passing genital urging. Why else would Burt have taken up with a gorgeous blond cocktail waitress, forgetting that, for all practical purposes, he already had one at home? Permissiveness, according to the theory, makes us contemptuous of such "traditional values" as loyalty, self-sacrifice, and the old death-do-us-part type of marriage.

The truth, I think, is that Americans love marriage too much. We rush into marriage with abandon, expecting a micro-Utopia on earth. We pile all our needs onto it, our expectations, neuroses, and hopes. In fact, we've made marriage into the panda bear of human social institutions: we've loved it to death.

Consider that marriage probably originated as a straightforward food-for-sex deal among foraging primates. Compatibility was not a big issue, nor, of course, was there any tension over who would control the remote. Today, however, a spouse is expected to be not only a co-provider and mate but a co-parent, financial partner, romantic love object, best friend, fitness adviser, home-repair person, and scintillating companion through the wasteland of Sunday afternoons. This is, rationally speaking, more than any one spouse can provide.

Probably the overload began with the Neolithic revolution, when males who were used to a career of hunting and bragging were suddenly required to stay home and help out with the crops. Then came the modern urban-industrial era, with the unprecedented notion of the "companionate marriage." Abruptly, the two sexes—which had gone for millennia without exchanging any more than the few grunts required for courtship—were expected to entertain each other with witty repartee over dinner.

Marriage might still have survived if it had not been for the sexual revolution and the radical new notion that one's helpmeet in life should, in addition to everything else, possess erotic skills formerly known only to gigolos and ladies of the night. Conversation had been a challenging enough demand; now anxious spouses were forced to master concepts like "G-spot" and "excitation plateau." No one thought it odd that the person who mowed your lawn or folded your shirts was now expected to provide orgasmic experiences at night.

In what other area of life would we demand that any one person fulfill such a huge multiplicity of needs? No one would think of asking his or her accountant to come by and prune the shrubbery, or the pediatrician to take out the garbage.

Everywhere else we observe a strict division of labor; only in marriage do we demand the all-purpose, multivalent Renaissance person.

Naturally, it doesn't work. The person who showed such ingenuity in bed turns out to be useless with a checkbook. The stud-muffin who looked so good in the gym reveals himself to be a libidoless couch warmer. Inevitably, we stray. But the American love of marriage is so gripping and deep that we are almost incapable of the discreet, long-term European-style affair. If spouse No. 1 fails in some realm of endeavor—sex, for example, or home repairs—we rush off in search of No. 2. The marriage-saving concept of "a little something on the side" is held to be immoral, un-American, and antithetical to "family values."

To put the whole thing in anthropological perspective: what we lack is not "values" but the old-fashioned neighborhood or community. Once, people found companionship among their old high school buddies, and got help with child raising from granddads and aunts. Marriages lasted because less was expected of them. If you wanted a bridge partner or a plumber or a confidant, you had a whole village to choose from. Today we don't marry a person—i.e., an actual human being, with all the attendant failings and limits—we attempt to marry a village.

The solution is to have separate "marriages" for separate types of marital functions. For example, a gay man of my acquaintance has entered into a co-parenting arrangement with two lesbian women. He will be a father to their collective child without any expectation that he will be a lover to the child's mothers or, for that matter, a jogging companion or co–mortgage holder. Child raising, in other words, has been cleanly separated from the turbulent realm of sex—which can only be good for the child. Or consider my relationship to the plumber. He dashes over whenever a pipe bursts, but there is no expectation of sex or profound emotional sharing. Consequently, ours is a "marriage" that works.

Of course, there will be religious objections to the new notion of multiple, simultaneous "marriages." Purists will quibble over what kind of vow is appropriate to make to one's accountant or fitness trainer. Jealousies may arise among the various individuals designated as one's sex partner, co-parent, dinner companion, and so forth. But in the end it will be worth it. All our needs will be met by individuals who are actually qualified to fulfill them. And we will all, maybe even Loni and Burt, go happily into the great ever-after.

[1993]

Want a Child?

Take My Son

The only good thing about the baby Jessica case is that they refrained from splitting her, Solomon-style, right down the middle. Apparently the judges agonized for weeks and only narrowly ruled out an ounce-by-ounce surgical distribution of the baby among the claimants. Instead, they decided to go with the ancient Law of DNA, which says that children should be as genetically similar to their parents as possible. This, of course, makes perfectly good sense if you are raising those children to be a source of transplantable organs—heart, kidney, liver, etc.—for your own eventual use.

But if you have any other purpose in raising a family, there is no reason to pay attention to the Law of DNA, which originated in the era of pterodactyls and lava pools. Consider: there are 5.7 billion people on earth today, many of them still at the drool-soaked, incontinent stage so appealing to would-be parents. Of these, millions are unclaimed orphans; at least orphans are numerous enough that in Rio de Janiero, for example, off-duty policemen are said to shoot them for sport. Could not some of those excess Brazilian street children have been shipped to Jessica's bio-parents, the Schmidts, instead of Jessica, who already had two enthusiastic parents on duty?

Then there are all the thousands of affluent, unorphaned American children whose parents, for one reason or another, can no longer afford to care for them. Take my son—as the comedians used to say in the borscht belt—please.

Yes, Mr. and Mrs. Schmidt, take him, and send Jessica home to the de Boers. All right, he's a little older than what you had in mind, but we are not talking about secondhand goods. My son is a fine, upstanding college student. He is not one of those fraternity types whose idea of a good time involves gang rapes and bouts of projectile vomiting. Nor is he some freak you don't dare kiss good-night for fear of being impaled on the nose jewelry. In fact, when he was Jessica's age, everyone wanted him. Strangers would come up on the street and say, "Hey, how much for that good-lookin' white kid in the stroller?" And I would, of course, be deeply flattered and mention what I took to be a reasonable sum. But let a child develop some expensive disease or learning disorder—or, as in my case, let him be accepted at one of our nation's finest Ivy League universities—and suddenly there are no more rival sets of parents to be found.

Do the Schmidts or the Twiggs (who are battling for switched-at-birth bio-daughter Kimberly in Florida) realize that the flip side of the Child as Genetic Property is the Child as Perpetual Liability? Have they been to The Gap to get an estimate of what it costs to minimally outfit a child or teen? Do they have any idea how much therapy their reluctant daughters are likely to need, not to mention orthodontia and family-planning visits? Are they aware of the bail required for your typical minor drug or driving infraction? Do they fully understand that, if worst comes to worst and things get totally out of hand, Jessica may someday even want to go to college?

Just as with the older child, I did everything possible to curb my son's academic ambitions. I tore up his homework whenever I could find it. I offered him funny-smelling cigarettes to smoke. I left brochures around the house promoting careers in landscaping, sanitation, and the bicycle-courier profession. I sent his résumé to Colin Powell.

Still, I was proud, in a morbid fashion, when he was accepted at a university so cutting-edge and intellectually advanced that you can be marked down for spelling "reality" without the quote marks. Naturally, I tried sending them "$25,000" instead of the first year's tuition, but this postmodern witticism fell flat in the university's business office. Desperately, I called and argued that I barely knew the boy and that for Mother's Day, year after year, he had always managed to find a lovely floral-decorated card with the chilling inscription: "You've been like a mother to me."

Furthermore, I told them I doubted that I was his actual bio-mother, what with all this switching at birth. He could, for all I knew, be Kimberly or Jessica, who each have two sets of potential parents to bill. But the university officials only smiled maliciously and said, "Sorry, we've got the DNA tests to prove that he's yours within a one percent margin of error. Send $25,000 without the quote marks, or we'll be coming by to take away the furniture."

Hence my implacable opposition to the Law of DNA. It distracts people like the Schmidts and the Twiggs from the millions of poor children who might actually have some use for their loving attentions. It forces them to focus these attentions on the minute number of children they are biochemically related to, even when those children want nothing to do with them. And, what is infinitely worse, the Law of DNA also restricts each child to a maximum of only two parents. Maybe two was enough in the old days, when all you really needed from a parent was a viable DNA strand. But—with college tuitions approaching the median family income—we need a whole new approach to the legal definition of kin.

So here is my solution: Send Jessica home to the only parents she knows. And as for the Schmidts and the Twiggs and all those other couples who are yearning for the vivid and moving experience of bio-parenthood—they can start by sending me a check.

[1993]

Cultural Baggage

An acquaintance was telling me about the joys of redis-
covering her ethnic and religious heritage. "I know exactly
what my ancestors were doing 2,000 years ago," she said, eyes
gleaming with enthusiasm, "and I can *do the same things now*."
Then she leaned forward and inquired politely, "And what is
your ethnic background, if I may ask?"

"None," I said, that being the first word in line to get out
of my mouth. Well, not "none," I backtracked. Scottish, English, Irish—that was something, I supposed. Too much Irish
to qualify as a WASP, too much of the hated English to warrant
a "Kiss Me, I'm Irish" button; plus there are a number of dead
ends in the family tree due to adoptions, missing records,
failing memories, and the like. I was blushing by this time.
Did "none" mean I was rejecting my heritage out of Anglo-
Celtic self-hatred? Or was I revealing a hidden chauvinism in
which the Britannically-derived serve as a kind of neutral standard compared to the ethnic "others"?

Throughout the sixties and seventies I watched one group
after another—African Americans, Latinos, Native Americans—stand up and proudly reclaim their roots while I just
sank back ever deeper into my seat. All this excitement over

ethnicity stemmed, I realized, from a past in which *their* ancestors had been trampled upon by *my* ancestors, or at least by
people who looked very much like them. In addition, it had
begun to seem almost un-American not to have some sort of
hyphen in hand, linking one to more venerable times and
locales.

But the truth is I was raised with "none." We'd eaten ethnic
foods in my childhood home, but these were all borrowed,
like the pasties, or Cornish meat pies, my father had picked
up from his fellow miners in Butte. If my mother had one
rule, it was militant ecumenicism in all matters of food and
experience: "Try new things," she would say, meaning anything from sweetbreads to clams, with an emphasis on the
"new."

As a child, I briefly nourished a craving for roots. I immersed
myself in the works of Sir Walter Scott. I pretended to believe
the bagpipe was a musical instrument. I was fascinated to learn
from a grandmother that we were descended from certain
Highland clans, and I longed for a pleated skirt in one of their
distinctive tartans.

But in *Ivanhoe* it was the dark-eyed "Jewess" Rebecca I
identified with, not the flaxen-haired bimbo Rowena. As for
clans: why not call them "tribes," those bands of half-clad
peasants and warriors whose idea of cuisine was stuffed sheep
gut washed down with whiskey? And then there was the sting
of Disraeli's remark, which I came across in my teens, to the
effect that his ancestors had been leading orderly, literate lives
when my ancestors were still daubing themselves with blue
paint.

Motherhood put the screws on me, ethnicity-wise. I had
hoped that by marrying a man of Eastern European–Jewish
descent I would acquire for my descendants the ethnic genes
that my own forebears so sadly lacked. At one point I even

subjected the children to a seder of my own design, including a little talk about the flight from Egypt and its relevance to modern social issues. But the kids insisted on buttering their matzohs and snickering through the sermon. "Give us a break, Mom," they said. "You don't even believe in God."

After the tiny pagans had been put to bed, I lit a cigarette and sat down to brood over Elijah's wine. What had I been thinking? The kids knew that their Jewish grandparents were secular folks who didn't do seders themselves. And if ethnicity eluded me, how could I expect it to take root in my children, who are not only Scottish-English-Irish but Hungarian-Polish-Russian to boot?

But then, on the fumes of Manischewitz, a great insight took form in my mind. It was true, as the kids said, that I didn't "believe in God." But this could be taken as something very different from an accusation—a reminder of a genuine heritage. My parents had not believed in God either, nor had my grandparents or any other progenitors going back to the great-great level. They had become disillusioned with Christianity generations ago—just as, on the in-law side, my children's other ancestors had shaken off their Orthodox Judaism. This insight did not exactly furnish me with an "identity," but it was something at least to work with: we are the kind of people, I realized—whatever our distant ancestors' religions —who do *not* believe, who do not carry on traditions, who do not do things just because someone has done them before.

The epiphany went on: I recalled that my mother never introduced a domestic procedure by telling me, "Grandma did it this way." What did Grandma know, living in the days before vacuum cleaners and disposable toilet mops? In my parents' general view, new things were better than old, and the very fact that some ritual had been performed in the past was a good reason for abandoning it now. Because what was the past, as our forebears knew it? Nothing but poverty, superstition, and grief. "Think for yourself," Dad used to say. "Always ask why."

In fact, this may have been the ideal cultural heritage for an ethnic strain like my own—bounced as it was from the Highlands of Scotland across the sea, then across the plains to the Rockies, down into the mines, and finally spewed out into high-tech, suburban America. What better philosophy, for a race of migrants, than "Think for yourself"? What better maxim, for a people whose whole world was rudely inverted every thirty years or so, than "Try new things"?

The more tradition-minded, the newly enthusiastic celebrants of Purim and Kwanzaa and Solstice, will be clucking sadly as they read this. They will see little point to survival if the survivors carry no cultural freight—religion, for example, or ethnic tradition. To which I would say that skepticism, curiosity, and wide-eyed ecumenical tolerance are also part of the human tradition, and are at least as old as such notions as "Serbian" or "Croatian," "Scottish" or "Jewish." I make no claims for my personal line of progenitors except that they remained steadfastly loyal to the values that induced all of our ancestors, long, long ago, to climb down from the trees and make their way into the open savanna.

A few weeks ago, I cleared my throat and asked the children, now mostly grown and fearsomely smart, whether they felt any stirrings of ethnic identity, etc., which might have been, ahem, insufficiently nourished at home. "None," they said, adding firmly, "and the world would be a better place if nobody else did either." My chest swelled with pride, as my mother's would have, to know that the race of "none" marches on.

[1992]

Housework

Is Obsolescent

It's been such a quiet revolution that you could hear a sock drop on a carpeted floor. Only you probably wouldn't pay any attention if you did.

Because what's one more sock down there among the broken action figures, lost homework papers, and fresh kills brought in by the cat? After decades of unappreciated drudgery, American women just don't do housework anymore—that is, beyond the minimum that is required in order to clear a path from the bedroom to the front door so they can get off to work in the morning.

There should have been a lot more fanfare for such a revolutionary change in the way that we live. If Americans suddenly gave up forks and started eating with their fingers, you can bet that would at least rate the "style section." But Harvard economist Juliet Schor's research shows that women have been eliminating a half hour of housework for every hour they work outside the home—or up to twenty hours a week, which is the equivalent of a 50-foot mound of unfolded laundry or a dust ball as large as a house.

Recall that not long ago, in our mothers' day, the standards were cruel but clear: every room should look like a motel room, only cleaner under the bed. The floors must be immaculate enough to double as plates, in case the guests prefer to eat doggie-style. The kitchen counters should be clean enough for emergency surgery, should the need at some time arise, and the walls should ideally be sterile. The alternative, we all learned in home economics, is the deadly scorn of the neighbors and probably plague.

For me, the turning point came when I realized that children don't eat off of walls. Food may end up on the walls, through processes of propulsion or skillful application with tiny fingers and palms, but once there, it is rarely ingested. And low to the ground as they are, children hardly ever even eat off of floors. In fact, a careful review of their eating habits reveals that the only surfaces you have to worry about, plague-wise, are the ones in McDonald's and Pizza Hut.

It had to happen sooner or later, this quiet revolt. Housework-as-we-know-it is not something ordained by the limits of the human immune system. It was invented, in fact, around the turn of the century for the precise purpose of giving middle-class women something to do. Once food processing and garment manufacture moved out of the home and into the factories, middle-class homemakers found themselves staring uneasily into the void. Should they join the suffragists? Go out in the work world and compete with the men? "Too many women," editorialized the *Ladies' Home Journal* in 1911, "are dangerously idle."

Enter the domestic-science experts, a group of ladies who, if ever there is a feminist hell, will be tortured eternally with feather dusters. These were women who made careers out of telling other women they couldn't have careers, because housework was a big enough job in itself. And they were right, since their standard for a well-kept home was one that revealed no evidence of human occupation.

Today, of course, the woman who opts to spend her days

polishing banisters is likely to soon find herself in foreclosure. If it's a choice between having food on the table or floors that are free of organic detritus, most of us choose to go with the food. And since child raising generally works better when children and parents share the same dwelling, there's no point in striving for the motel look.

We all know, or suspect, that after you eliminate the T-shirt ironing and the weekly changing of sheets, there will still be some biological minimum below which no family dares go. In the meantime, each chore has to be carefully assessed: If you don't do the toilets, will the children get typhoid? Which is easier anyway—doing all that scrubbing, or taking a little time now and then to visit one's family members in the infectious-disease ward?

For any man or child who misses the pristine standards of yesteryear, there is a simple solution—pitch in! Surveys show men doing more than they used to, but nowhere near enough to maintain the old standards. The technology of the vacuum cleaner is challenging, I admit, but not beyond the capacity of the masculine mind.

Or maybe we should just relax and enjoy the revolution. Here was a form of human toil that was said to be immutable and biologically necessary: social convention demanded it, advertisers of household products promoted it, mothers-in-law enforced it. But we cut back drastically, and, lo, the kids are as healthy as ever—maybe more so now that we have a little more time to hang out with them.

How many other forms of "necessary" labor may also turn out to be ritual, designed to keep us homebound and politically passive? Checkbook balancing, for example. Isn't it time we acknowledged that the bank is always right and, even when it's not, that it's bound to win anyway? Or saving the invoices from last year's bills, in case the canceled checks get destroyed in a meteor hit. Are you ever, in the twilight of life, going to ask yourself, "Gee, what did I spend on heating fuel in the winter of '92?"

It's even occurred to me, as a teeny little subversive whisper of a thought, that if we stop mowing the lawn right now, it will probably be a long, long time before the yard gets overrun by lions and snakes.

[1993]

The Wretched of

the Hearth

In the second half of the 1980s, when American conservatism had reached its masochistic zenith with the reelection of Ronald Reagan, when women's liberation had been replaced by the more delicate sensibility known as postfeminism, when everyone was a yuppie and the heartiest word of endorsement in our vocabulary was "appropriate," there was yet this one paradox: our favorite TV personages were a liberal black man and a left-wing white feminist. Cosby could be explained as a representative of America's officially profamily mood, but Roseanne is a trickier case. Her idea of humor is to look down on her sleeping family in the eponymous sitcom and muse, "Mmmm, I wonder where we could find an all-night taxidermist."

If zeitgeist were destiny, Roseanne would never have happened. Only a few years ago, we learn from her autobiography, *Roseanne: My Life As a Woman*, Roseanne Arnold was just your run-of-the-mill radical feminist mother-of-three, writing poems involving the Great Goddess, denouncing all known feminist leaders as sellout trash, and praying for the sixties to be born again in a female body. Since the entertainment media do not normally cast about for fat, loudmouthed feminists to promote to superstardom, we must assume that Roseanne has something to say that many millions of people have been waiting to hear. Like this, upon being told of a woman who stabbed her husband thirty-seven times: "I admire her restraint."

Roseanne is the neglected underside of the American female experience, bringing together the great themes of poverty, obesity, and defiance. The overside is handled well enough by Candice Bergen (*Murphy Brown*) and Madonna, who exist to remind us that talented women who work out are bound to become fabulously successful. Roseanne works a whole different beat, both in her sitcom and in the movie *She-Devil*, portraying the hopeless underclass of the female sex: polyester-clad, overweight occupants of the slow track; fast-food waitresses, factory workers, housewives, members of the invisible pink-collar army; the despised, the jilted, the underpaid.

Not that *Roseanne* is free of class stereotyping. The Connors must bear part of the psychic burden imposed on all working-class people by their economic and occupational betters: they inhabit a zone of glad-handed gemeinschaft, evocative, now and then, of the stock wedding scene (*The Godfather, The Deer Hunter, Working Girl*) that routinely signifies lost old-world values. They indulge in a manic physicality that would be unthinkable among the more controlled and genteel Huxtables. They maintain a traditional, low-fiber diet of white bread and macaroni. They are not above a fart joke.

Still, in *Roseanne* I am willing to forgive the stereotypes as markers designed to remind us of where we are: in the home of a construction worker and his minimum-wage wife. Without the reminders, we might not be aware of how thoroughly the deeper prejudices of the professional class are being challenged. Roseanne's fictional husband Dan (played by the irresistibly cuddly John Goodman) drinks domestic beer and dedicates Sundays to football; but far from being a Bunkeresque boor, he looks to this feminist like the fabled "sensitive man" we have all been pining for. He treats his rotund wife like a sex goddess. He picks up on small cues signaling emotional distress. He helps with homework. And when Roseanne works overtime, he cooks, cleans, and rides herd on the kids without any of the piteous whining we have come to expect from upscale males in their rare, and lavishly documented, encounters with soiled Pampers.

Roseanne Connor has her own way of defying the stereotypes. Variously employed as a fast-food operative, a factory worker, a bartender, and a telephone salesperson, her real dream is to be a writer. When her twelve-year-old daughter Darlene (brilliantly played by Sara Gilbert) balks at a poetry-writing assignment, Roseanne gives her a little talking-to involving Sylvia Plath: "She inspired quite a few women, including *moi*." In another episode, a middle-aged friend thanks Roseanne for inspiring her to dump her chauvinist husband and go to college. We have come a long way from the dithering, cowering Edith Bunker.

Most of the time the Connors do the usual sitcom things. They have the little domestic misunderstandings that can be patched up in twenty-four minutes with wisecracks and a round of hugs. But *Roseanne* carries working-class verisimilitude into a new and previously taboo dimension—the workplace. In the world of employment, Roseanne knows exactly where she stands: "All the good power jobs are taken. Vanna turns the letters. Leona's got hotels. Margaret's running England . . . 'Course she's not doing a very good job . . ."

And in the workplace as well as the kitchen, Roseanne knows how to dish it out. A friend of mine, herself a denizen of the low-wage end of the work force, claims to have seen an episode in which Roseanne led an occupational-health-and-safety battle at Wellman Plastics. I missed that one, but I have seen her, on more than one occasion, reduce the boss's ego to rubble. At Chicken Divine, for example, she is ordered to work weekends—an impossibility for a working mother—by an officious teenage boss who confides that he doesn't like working weekends either. In a sequence that could have been crafted by Michael Moore, Roseanne responds: "Well, that's real good 'cause you never do. You sit in your office like a little Napoleon, making up schedules and screwing up people's lives." To which he says, "That's what they pay me for. And you are paid to follow my orders." Blah blah blah. To which she says, after staring at him fixedly for several seconds: "You know, you got a little prize hanging out of your nose there."

All family sitcoms, of course, teach us that wisecracks and swift put-downs are the preferred modes of affectionate discourse. But Roseanne takes the genre a step further—over the edge, some may say. In the era of big weddings and sudden man shortages, she describes marriage as "a life sentence, without parole." And in the era of the biological time clock and the petted yuppie midlife baby, she can tell Darlene to get a fork out of the drawer and "stick it through your tongue." Or she can say, when Dan asks "Are we missing an offspring?" at breakfast, "Yeah. Where do you think I got the bacon?"

It is Roseanne's narrow-eyed cynicism about the family, even more than her class consciousness, that gives *Roseanne* its special frisson. Archie Bunker got our attention by telling us that we (blacks, Jews, "ethnics," WASPs, etc.) don't really like each other. Roseanne's message is that even within the family we don't much like each other. We *love* each other (who else do we have?); but The Family, with its lopsided division of labor and its ancient system of age-graded humiliations, just doesn't work. Or rather, it doesn't work unless the contradictions are smoothed out with irony and the hostilities are periodically blown off as humor. Coming from Mom, rather than from a jaded teenager or a bystander dad, this is scary news indeed.

So Roseanne's theoretical outlook is, in the best left-feminist tradition, dialectical. On the one hand, she presents the family as a zone of intimacy and support, well worth defending against the forces of capitalism, which drive both mothers and fathers out of the home, scratching around for paychecks. On the other hand, the family is hardly a haven, especially for its grown-up females. It is marred from within by—among other things—the patriarchal division of leisure, which makes Dad and the kids the "consumers" of Mom's cooking, cleaning, nurturing, and (increasingly) her earnings. Mom's job is to keep the whole thing together—to see that the mortgage payments are made, to fend off the viperish teenagers, to find the missing green sock—but Mom is no longer interested in being a human sacrifice on the altar of "profamily values." She's been down to the feminist bookstore; she's been reading Sylvia Plath.

This is a bleak and radical vision. Not given to didacticism, Roseanne offers no programmatic ways out. Surely, we are led to conclude, pay equity would help, along with child care, and so on. But Roseanne leaves us hankering for a quality of change that goes beyond mere reform: for a world in which even the lowliest among us—the hash slinger, the sock finder, the factory hand—will be recognized as the poet she truly is.

[1990]

Sex and the

Married Woman

There are truths that bear repeating at least once a generation, and one of them, apparently, is that adultery is not a capital offense. It was exactly thirty years ago that Helen Gurley Brown announced in her protofeminist manifesto, *Sex and the Single Girl*, that "nice girls *do* have affairs, and they do not necessarily die of them!" Now a new study by social observer Dalma Heyn shows that married women, too, can have affairs and live to tell the tale—with gusto, in fact, and in titillating detail. Among the adulteresses interviewed by Heyn for her book *The Erotic Silence of the American Wife*, none committed suicide, developed a debilitating sexual obsession, or crumpled to the floor with a sexually transmitted disease. Amazingly, in an era when we seldom hear of an attraction that is not preceded by the warning word "fatal," adultery seems to have had much the same impact on these women as a week at a four-star spa: they report feeling vital, alert, and transcendentally sexy.

Not that the issue of fatality is anything to take lightly, even aside from the menace of AIDS. Depending on the culture, Heyn reports, an adulterous woman may be gang-raped, speared in the leg, branded with a fire stick, or simply killed.

In Saudi Arabia, adulterous wives are stoned to death. In Brazil, husbands were routinely acquitted for murdering straying wives until the late 1970s, when feminists rose up in protest.

In those parts of the world where public stonings are frowned upon, great literature has stepped in to fill the gap. Tolstoy threw Anna Karenina under a train, Madame Bovary was dispatched with arsenic, and poor Hester Prynne soldiered on with an "A" on her chest. From *Tess of the D'Urbervilles* to Mary McCarthy's A *Charmed Life*, the message to the well-read woman is that she has three sexual options: monogamy, celibacy—or death.

Then there is the current, postfeminist orthodoxy which holds that males need abundant and varied sex while women crave only warm, cuddly, committed love. Hence the widespread irritation at celebrity victims Anita Hill, Patricia Bowman, and Desiree Washington: men are beasts, according to the new Victorianism, at the mercy of their gonads. It's up to the woman, with her far lower lust level, to draw a firm line in the sand. Any woman who fails to do so—or, worse yet, defies the orthodoxy by bouncing from bed to bed—is widely believed to deserve what she gets.

But according to surveys Heyn cites, somewhere between 26 and 41 percent of married women are unfaithful. Most of the women in Heyn's sample (which is admittedly tiny and narrow—all apparently white, educated, and upper-middle-class) are busy, creative people blessed with reasonably happy marriages. With one or two exceptions, they remain with their husbands, even enriching their marriages with the sensuality and emotional intensity they have recaptured through their erotic adventures. Where are the suicides, the critics will no doubt demand, the *Fatal Attraction*–style boilers-of-rabbits, the remorseful self-flagellants?

Now I may be old-fashioned, but it seems to me we should

be beyond all this—beyond the controversy Heyn's book is bound to stir up and the need for the book itself. We did, after all, have a sexual revolution, and it was much more than a tempest in Hugh Hefner's hot tub. Sex pioneers like Virginia Johnson and Germaine Greer tossed out the old myths of female frigidity and innate monogamy. Nancy Friday published our naughtiest fantasies. We had whole conferences about sex back in those days, when the word didn't require the prefix "safe."

I remember a feminist conference on sexuality that I attended in 1975. There were workshops on masturbation, a speaker who confessed to lusting after her gynecologist, and many proud advocates of casual and varied sex. Adultery, if the word ever came up, would have been dismissed as an archaic usage and an insipid concept, politically far from correct. Who, after all, had mentioned marriage? We were gathered for the contemplation of *sex*, and, for the first time in many women's personal histories, sex as something other than plumbing or masochism. For a few brief moments there in the seventies, we glimpsed an entirely new vision of ourselves: as multiorgasmic, polymorphously inclined beings rushing open-armed into the world, confident, desirous, trusting.

Ah, how fleeting that vision was! In the years immediately following, feminists shifted their focus from sex to sexual violence, from cunnilingus to karate. A new generation of thirty-five-year-olds started watching the biological time clock and scheduling sex, when they had it, by the thermometer reading. Former sexual liberationists cringed before the onslaught of the Christian right, with its demands, for example, that family planning clinics be replaced by "chastity centers." And then, of course, there was AIDS. The speakers from that 1975 conference have probably long since checked into recovery programs for the sexually overwrought.

But the sexual counterrevolution of the eighties didn't lead to the "end of sex," as a 1982 *Esquire* cover story claimed, only to the renaissance of old-time hypocrisy. Bill Clinton: a married man having *affairs*? Clarence Thomas: a rising young lawyer with a taste for pornography? Nooo. We follow the celebrity rape cases right down to the panty hose and Lightdays pads and then scream at the media for serving us smut. In this context, even mild offenders—ordinary married women conducting lunch-hour affairs with nice fellows they meet through their jobs—begin to seem like death-defying rebels.

So *The Erotic Silence of the American Wife* is a far more important and revolutionary book than it would have been a mere fifteen years ago—or in any culture that has achieved some measure of sexual honesty. Heyn stops short of advocating affairs or suggesting that marriage, with its sexually anesthetic effects, may be an institution in need of profound renovation. But she does remind us, in intelligent, reflective tones, that women are sexual beings and that, for women as well as men, sex is fundamentally a lawless creature, not easily confined to a cage.

[1992]

The Economics

of Cloning

Any normal species would be delighted at the prospect of cloning. No more nasty surprises like sickle-cell anemia or Down's syndrome—just batch after batch of high-grade and, genetically speaking, immortal offspring! But representatives of the human species are responding as if someone had proposed adding satanism to the grade-school curriculum. Suddenly, perfectly secular folks are throwing around words like "sanctity" and dredging up medieval-era arguments against the hubris of science. No one has proposed burning him at the stake, but the poor fellow who induced a human embryo to double itself has virtually recanted—proclaiming his reverence for human life in a voice, *Time* magazine reported, "choking with emotion."

There is an element of hypocrisy to much of the anticloning furor, or, at best, superstition. The fact is we are already well down the path leading to genetic manipulation of the creepiest sort. Life-forms can be patented, which means they can be bought and sold and potentially traded on the commodities markets. Human embryos are life-forms, and there is nothing to stop anyone from marketing them now, on the same shelf with the Cabbage Patch dolls.

In fact, any culture that encourages in vitro fertilization has no right to complain about a market in embryos. The assumption behind the in vitro industry is that some people's genetic material is worth more than others' and deserves to be reproduced at any expense. Millions of low-income babies die every year from preventable ills like dysentery, while heroic efforts go into maintaining yuppie zygotes in test tubes at the unicellular stage. This is the dread "nightmare" of eugenics in familiar, marketplace form—which involves breeding the best-paid instead of the "best."

Cloning technology is an almost inevitable by-product of in vitro fertilization. Once you decide to go to the trouble of in vitro, with its potentially hazardous megadoses of hormones for the female partner and various indignities for the male, you might as well make a few back-up copies of any viable embryo that's produced. And once you've got the back-up copies, it's a skip and hop to deciding to keep a few in the freezer, in case Junior ever needs a new kidney or cornea.

No one much likes the idea of thawing out one of the clone-kids to harvest its organs, but according to Andrew Kimbrell, author of *The Human Body Shop*, in the last few years an estimated fifty to one hundred couples have produced babies to provide tissue for an existing child. Plus there's already a thriving market in third-world kidneys and eyes. Is growing your own really so much worse than plundering the bodies of the poor? Or maybe we'll just clone for the fun of it. If you like a movie scene, you can rewind the tape; so when Junior gets all pimply and nasty, why not start over with Junior II? Sooner or later, at least among the in vitro class, instant replay will be considered a human right.

The existential objections ring a little bit hollow. How will it feel to be one clone among hundreds? the anticloners ask. Probably no worse than it feels to be the three-millionth thirteen-year-old dressed in identical baggy trousers, untied sneakers, and baseball cap—a feeling usually described as "cool." In mass consumer society, notions like "precious individuality" are best reserved for the Nike ads.

Besides, if we truly believed in the absolute uniqueness of each individual, there would be none of this unseemly eagerness to reproduce one's own particular genome. What is it, after all, that drives people to in vitro fertilization rather than adoption? Deep down, we don't want to believe that we are each unique, one-time-only events in the universe. We hope to happen again, and again. And when the technology arrives for cloning adult individuals, genetic immortality should be within reach of the average multimillionaire. Ross Perot will be followed by a flock of little re-Rosses.

As for the argument that the clones will be subpeople, existing to gratify the vanity of their parents (or their "originals," as the case may be): since when has it been illegal to use one person as a vehicle for the ambitions of another? If we don't yet breed children for their SAT scores, there is a whole class of people, heavily overlapping with the in vitro class, who coach their toddlers to get into the nursery schools that offer a fast track to Harvard. You don't have to have been born in a test tube to be an extension of someone else's ego.

For that matter, if we get serious about the priceless uniqueness of each individual, many venerable social practices will have to go. It's hard to see why people should be able to sell their labor, for example, but not their embryos or eggs. Labor is also made out of the precious stuff of life—energy and cognition and so forth—which is hardly honored when "unique individuals" by the millions are condemned to mind-killing, repetitive work.

The critics of cloning say we should know what we're getting into, with all its Orwellian implications. But if the critics prevail and we decide to outlaw cloning, we should understand the implications of *that*. We would be saying, in effect, that we prefer to leave genetic destiny to the crapshoot of nature —despite sickle cell and Tay-Sachs and all the rest—because ultimately we don't trust the market to regulate life itself. And this may be the hardest thing of all to acknowledge: that it is not just twenty-first-century technology we fear but the centuries-old economics of Adam Smith.

[1993]

Fun with Cults

"Tell us the one about Luc Jouret and the Solar Temple cult!" the children squeal eagerly as bedtime approaches. We have been watching the cult experts on CNN, marveling at these morose, gray-suited fellows who make it their business to monitor the far fringes of human behavior, the kinky allegiances disdained by all normal adults. "Well, they put plastic baggies over their heads," I begin, to shrieks of wild delight. This is their favorite part, the ultimate frisson, since every child knows you must never, ever, wear a plastic baggie over your head, even if you're dressing for a ritual suicide—or homicide, as the case may turn out to be.

But the bedtime story does not go smoothly tonight. The children want to know what a "cult" is exactly and whether the Girl Scouts qualify. I explain that cults generally have some sort of suicide aspect, like Jonestown or those Waco folks who incinerated themselves with the assistance of the federal government. Then what about Weight Watchers? a child asks. Small groups of devotees, usually gathering by night, dedicated to mortifying the flesh?

No, I tell them, in addition to the suicide aspect, cults are required to have some religious or quasi-religious dimension as well. The exception would be Scientology, which, as its name implies, is the very opposite of a religion and is, in fact, a system for removing "engrams," or peculiar little blockages, from the minds of celebrities (Tom Cruise is a prominent member), along with money from their bank accounts. When one of these secular-type cults gets large enough, it is known as an "organization." Eventually, when the money-garnering techniques are perfected and the quasi-religious activities have been narrowed down to "motivational workshops," it may be referred to as a "corporation."

So naturally the children want to know the difference between a cult and a normal, God-fearing, tax-exempt religion. They have noticed the marked similarities, in the matter of robe-wearing for example, between officials of the Solar Temple and those of the Catholic Church. I respond by pointing out that there are many tiny distinctions, obvious to any theologian, such as the fact that the cultists worship a Jesus-figure with a rose hovering over His head, while real Christians prefer the hovering to be done by a dove, if not Jesus's own excised heart or some related blood-processing organ.

Besides, Christianity is about goodness and kindness and frolics with lambs, while cults tend to feature madness and self-destructive fury—as in baggies worn over the head. But now the children clamor to remind me of the thirteenth-century Catholic flagellation fad, whose adherents interrupted their self-torments only long enough to dispatch the occasional Jew. Not to mention the many fine saints like Mary Magdalene of Pazzi, who nourished herself on maggots sucked from ulcerous sores. There was even a time, the children remind me, when Christianity was reviled as a "cult" by all decent, ox-sacrificing pagans.

Thus cornered, I am forced to admit that the difference between a religion and a cult is chiefly a matter of size. Forty-eight people donning plastic bags and shooting themselves in the head is a "cult," while a hundred million people bowing before a flesh-hating elderly celibate is obviously a world-class religion. Similarly, a half-dozen Trotskyists meeting over coffee is a "sect," while a few million gun-toting, Armageddon-ready Baptists are referred to as the Republican Party.

It is the job of the government to distinguish the cults from the bona fide religions, I explain, and the government is the embodiment of the Nation. And the Nation? Well, the Nation is an invisible entity we belong to, a kind of special club for Americans, or Paraguayans, as the case may be, only far more serious than, say, your average secret society of ten-year-old boys. Good citizens stand ready to give their lives for the Nation, should their leaders request that they do so.

"Another cult!" the children howl in delight. And I sit there shamefaced, at a loss to explain how epaulets and crucifixes, rosaries and flags, differ substantively from plastic baggies and hovering roses.

[1994]

Oh, Those *Family Values*

A disturbing subtext runs through our recent media fixations. Parents abuse sons—allegedly, at least, in the Menendez case—who in turn rise up and kill them. A husband torments a wife, who retaliates, in the best-known case, with a kitchen knife. Love turns into obsession, between the Simpsons anyway, and then perhaps into murderous rage. The family, in other words, as personal hell.

This accounts for at least part of our fascination with the Bobbitts and the Simpsons and the rest of them. We live in a culture that fetishizes the family as the ideal unit of human community, the perfect container for our lusts and loves. Politicians of both parties are aggressively "profamily"; even abortion-rights bumper stickers proudly link "profamily" and "prochoice." Only with the occasional celebrity crime do we allow ourselves to think the nearly unthinkable: that the family may not be the ideal and perfect living arrangement after all —that it can also be a nest of pathology and a cradle of gruesome violence.

It's a scary thought, since the family is at the same time our "haven in a heartless world." Theoretically, and sometimes actually, the family nurtures warm, loving feelings, uncontaminated by greed or power hunger. Within the family, and often only within the family, individuals are loved "for themselves," and whether or not they are infirm, incontinent, infantile, or eccentric. The strong (adults and, especially, males) lie down peaceably with the small and the weak.

But consider the matter of wife battery. We managed to dodge it in the Bobbitt case and downplay it as a force in Tonya Harding's life. Thanks to O.J., though, we're caught up now in a mass consciousness-raising session, grimly absorbing the fact that in some areas domestic violence sends more women to emergency rooms than any other form of illness, injury, or assault.

Still, we shrink from the obvious inference: for a woman, home is, statistically speaking, the most dangerous place to be. Her worst enemies and potential killers are not strangers but lovers, husbands, and those who claimed to love her once. Similarly, for every Polly Klaas who is killed by a deranged criminal on parole, dozens of children are abused and murdered by their own parents, uncles, or stepfathers. Home is all too often where the small and the weak fear to lie down and shut their eyes.

At some deep, queasy Freudian level we all know this. Even in the ostensibly "functional," nonviolent family, where no one is killed or maimed, feelings are routinely bruised and even twisted out of shape. There is the slap or put-down that violates a child's shaky sense of self; the cold, distracted stare that drives a spouse to tears; the little digs and rivalries. At best, the family teaches the finest things human beings can learn from one another—generosity and love. But it is also, all too often, where we learn nasty things like hate and rage and shame.

Americans act out their ambivalence about the family without ever owning up to it. Millions adhere to creeds—religious and political—that are militantly "profamily." But at the same time, millions flock to therapists and self-help groups that offer to heal the "inner child" from damage inflicted by family life. Legions of women band together to revive the self-esteem they lost in supposedly loving relationships and to learn to love a little less. We are all, it is often said, "in recovery." And from what? Our families, in most cases.

There is a long and honorable tradition of what might be called "antifamily" thought. The early-nineteenth-century French philosopher Charles Fourier taught that the family was a barrier to human progress and encouraged the formation of family-free alternative communities. Early feminists saw a degrading parallel between marriage and prostitution, and challenged the patriarchal authority of the husband/father. In the 1960s, radical psychiatrists denounced the family as a hotbed of neurosis, and the renowned British anthropologist Edmund Leach stated that "far from being the basis of the good society, the family, with its narrow privacy and tawdry secrets, is the source of all our discontents."

But communes proved harder to sustain than plain old couples, and the conservatism of the 1980s crushed the last vestiges of "lifestyle experimentation." Today, even gays and lesbians are eager to get married and take up family life. Feminists have learned to couch their concerns as "family issues," and public figures would sooner advocate crack-cocaine as a cure for stress than propose the family as a target for reform. Hence our unseemly interest in O.J., Erik, Lyle, and Lorena: they allow us, however gingerly, to break the silence on the hellish side of family life.

But the discussion needs to become a lot more open and forthright. We may be stuck with the family—at least until someone invents a sustainable alternative—but the family, with its deep, impacted tensions and longings, can hardly be expected to be the moral foundation of everything else. In fact, many families could use a lot more outside interference in the form of counseling and policing, and some are so dangerously dysfunctional that they ought to be encouraged to disband right away. Even healthy families need outside sources of moral guidance to keep those tensions from imploding—and this means, among other things, a public philosophy of gender equality and concern for child welfare. When, instead, the larger culture aggrandizes wife beaters, degrades women, or nods approvingly at child slappers, the family gets a little more dangerous for everyone, and so, inevitably, does the larger world.

[1994]

BODY

ISSUES

Why Don't We Like

the Human Body?

There's something wrong when a seven-dollar movie in the mall can leave you with posttraumatic stress syndrome. In the old days, killers merely stalked and slashed and strangled. Today they flay their victims and stash the rotting, skinless corpses. Or they eat them filleted, with a glass of wine, when there's time to cook—or live, with the skin still on, when there's only time for a snack. It's not even the body count that matters anymore. What counts is the number of ways to trash the body: decapitation, dismemberment, impalings, and (ranging into the realm of printed word) eye gougings, power drillings, and the application of hungry rodents to some poor victim's innards.

All right, terrible things do happen. Real life is filled with serial killers, mass murderers, and sickos of all degrees. Much of the twentieth century, it could be argued, has been devoted to the ingenious production and disposal of human corpses. But the scary thing is not that eye gougings and vivisections and meals of human flesh may, occasionally, happen. The scary thing, the thing that ought to make the heart pound and the skin go cold and tingly, is that somehow we find this fun to watch.

There's no shortage of theories to explain our addiction to violence and horror. In what might be called the testosterone theory, a congenital error in the wiring of the male brain leads to a confusion between violence and sex. Men get off on hideous mayhem, and women supposedly cover their eyes. Then there's the raging puritan theory, which is based on the statistical fact that those who get slashed or eaten in the movies are usually guilty of a little fooling around themselves. It's only a tingle of rectitude we feel, according to this, when the bad girl finally gets hers. There's even an invidious comparison theory: we enjoy seeing other people get sautéed or chainsawed because at least it's not happening to *us*.

The truth could be so much simpler that it's staring us in the face. There has always been a market for scary stories and vicarious acts of violence. But true horror can be bloodless, as in Henry James's matchless tale *The Turn of the Screw*, and even reckless violence, as in the old-time western, need not debauch the human form. No, if offerings like *American Psycho* and *The Silence of the Lambs* have anything to tell us about ourselves, it must be that, at this particular historical moment, we have come to hate the human body.

Think about it. Only a couple of decades ago, we could conceive of better uses for the body than as a source of meat or leather. Sex, for example. Sex was once considered a valid source of thrills even if both parties were alive and remained so throughout the act. Therapists urged us to "get in touch with our bodies"; feminists celebrated "our bodies, ourselves." Minimally, the body was a portable personal habitat that could be shared with special loved ones. Maximally, it was a powerhouse offering multiple orgasms and glowing mind-body epiphanies. Skin was something to massage or gently stroke.

Then, for good reasons and bad, we lost sex. It turned out to spread deadly viruses. It offended the born-again puritans. It led to messy entanglements that interfered with networking and power lunching. Since there was no way to undress for success, we switched in the mid-1980s to food. When we weren't eating, we were watching food-porn starring Julia Child or working off calories on the StairMaster. The body wasn't perfect, but it could, with effort and willpower, be turned into a lean, mean eating machine.

And then we lost food. First they took the red meat, the white bread, and the Chocolate Decadence desserts. Then they came for the pink meat, the cheese, the butter, the tropical oils, and, of course, the whipped cream. Finally they wanted all protein abolished, all fat and uncomplex carbohydrates, leaving us with broccoli and Metamucil as the only official food groups. Everything else, as we now know, is transformed by our treacherous bodies into insidious, slow-acting toxins.

So no wonder we enjoy seeing the human body being shredded, quartered, flayed, filleted, and dissolved in vats of acid. It let us down. No wonder we love heroes and megavillains like Robocop and the Terminator, in whom all soft, unreliable tissue has been replaced by metal alloys. Or that we like reading (even in articles that are, of course, deeply critical of the violence they manage to summarize) about diabolical new uses for human flesh. It's been, let's face it, a big disappointment. Might as well feed it to the rats or to any cannibalistically inclined killer still reckless enough to indulge in red meat.

But it's time for a truce with the soft and wayward flesh. Maybe violent imagery feeds the obsessions of real-life sickos. Or maybe, as some argue, it drains their sickness off into harmless fantasy. But surely it cheapens our sense of ourselves to think that others, even fictional others, could see us as little more than meat. And it's hard to believe that all this carnage doesn't dull our response to the global wastage of human flesh in famine, flood, and war.

We could start by admitting that our 1970s-era expectations were absurdly high. The body is not a reliable source of ecstasy or transcendent insight. For most of our lives, it's a shambling, jury-rigged affair, filled with innate tensions, contradictions, broken springs. Hollywood could help by promoting better uses for the body, like real sex, by which I mean sex between people who are often wrinkled and overweight and sometimes even fond of each other. The health meanies could relax and acknowledge that one of the most marvelous functions of the body is, in fact, to absorb small doses of whipped cream and other illicit substances.

Then maybe we could start making friends with our bodies again. They need nurturance and care, but, like any friend, they should be good for a romp now and then, by which I mean something involving dancing or petting, as opposed to dicing and flaying. But even "friends" is another weird and alienated image. The truth, which we have almost forgotten, is that Bodies "Я" Us.

[1991]

Stamping Out

a Dread Scourge

In the spirit of a public-health campaign, the American Society for Plastic and Reconstructive Surgery (ASPRS) has launched a PR drive to "tell the other side of the [breast-implant] story." Public health? Slicing women's chests open so that they can be stuffed with a close chemical relative of Silly Putty? Yes, indeed, because the plastic surgeons understand what the Food and Drug Administration is so reluctant to acknowledge: that small breasts are not just a harmless challenge to the bikini wearer or would-be topless entertainer. They are a disease, a disfiguring illness for which the technical term is *micromastia*.

As the ASPRS tried to explain to the FDA ten years ago, "there is a substantial and enlarging body of medical information and opinion to the effect that these deformities [small breasts] are really a disease." Not a fatal disease perhaps, to judge from the number of sufferers who are still hobbling around untreated, but a disease nonetheless, like flu or TB. And anyone tempted to fault the medical establishment for inaction on breast cancer or AIDS should consider its quiet, but no less heroic progress against the scourge of micromastia: in the last thirty years, 1.6 million victims have been identified, diagnosed, and cured. Who says our health system doesn't work?

Once we understand that small breasts are a "disease," it's easier to see why Dow Corning and others rushed so breathlessly to get their implants onto the market. Why diddle around with slow, costly tests while an epidemic is raging out there? And everyone's life is touched by the tragedy of micromastia because everyone has a friend, sister, co-worker, or wife who falls pitifully short in the mammary department. In the past, small groups of health-conscious males, typically gathered at construction sites, would offer free diagnoses to women passersby, but there was little that could be done until the advent of the insertable Silly Putty breast.

Admittedly, micromastia is in some ways an atypical disease. It is painless, which is why many victims put off treatment for years, and it in no way diminishes breast function, if that is still defined in the old-fashioned way as lactation. The implants, on the other hand, can interfere with lactation, and they make mammograms tricky to read (not to mention the occasional disfiguring or life-threatening side effect like lupus or scleroderma). But so what if micromastia has no functional impact? Why can't a disease be manifested solely by size?

Consider the rigorously scientific methods employed by the medical profession in its efforts to curb the epidemic. Not just anyone could get breast implants. No, the doctor had to study the afflicted area first to decide whether they were truly needed. A friend of mine, an inquiring journalist of average proportions, called a New York–area plastic surgeon to inquire about implants and was told to come in for an exam. One quick, searching look and he told her that, yes, she needed them, badly.

In fact, according to the tabloids, Jessica Hahn needed them too, as may have Melanie Griffith, Jane Fonda, Brigitte Nielsen, and even, gasp, Dolly Parton. Why take chances? The doctors know there are not only obvious forms of micromastia, discernable to the man on the street, but insidious, hidden forms—very well hidden indeed.

So we can see why the plastic surgeons were willing to cough up hundreds of dollars each to finance the ASPRS's campaign to show the bright side of the breast-implant story. Though nearly two million micromastia victims have been cured, millions more remain untreated, as shown by the continued existence of the plague's dread symbol—the A-cup bra. There have been many earnest attempts to reach the untreated: public-health-oriented magazines like *Playboy* repeatedly print photos illustrating normal breast size for the woman in doubt. Tragically though, many women still live in denial, concealing their condition under mannish blazers and suit jackets, forgoing the many topless forms of employment.

And we can see too why there was nothing sexist about American Medical Association spokesman Dr. Mitchell Karlin's warning that the recent moratorium on implants would cause "absolute hysteria among women." Look at those unruly AIDS and breast-cancer activists—why not a mass movement of micromastia victims, marching and chanting for immediate help?

Now, a cynic might see the silicone-implant business as another scam on the scale of the Dalkon Shield (which had a tendency to cause devastating infections), DES (which could cause cancer in the user's offspring), or the high-estrogen birth-control pill (which was also rushed to market after hasty and dubious testing). A cynic might point to the medical profession's long habit of exploiting the female body for profit— from the nineteenth-century custom of removing the ovaries as a cure for "hysteria," to our more recent traditions of unnecessary hysterectomies and cesareans. A cynic might conclude that the real purpose of the $500-million-a-year implant business is the implantation of fat in the bellies and rumps of underemployed plastic surgeons.

But our cynic would be missing the point of modern medical science. We may not have a cure for every disease, alas, but there's no reason we can't have a disease for every cure. With silicone implants, small breasts became micromastia. With injectable growth hormone, short kids become treatable dwarves. Plastic surgeons can now cure sagging jowls and chins, droopy eyelids and insufficiently imposing male chests and calves. So we can expect to hear soon about the menace of new diseases like saggy jowlitis, prolapsed eyelid, and hypo-pectoralis.

It will be hard, though, to come up with anything quite so convincing as micromastia. As the plastic surgeons must have realized, American culture is almost uniquely obsessed with large, nurturing bosoms. And with the silicone scandal upon us, we can begin to see why: in a society so unnurturing that even health care can be sadistically perverted for profit, people are bound to have a desperate, almost pathological need for the breast.

[1992]

The Naked Truth

about Fitness

The conversation has all the earmarks of a serious moral debate. The man is holding out for the pleasures of this life, few as they are and short as it is. The woman (we assume his wife, since they are having breakfast together and this is a prime-time television commercial) defends the high road of virtue and self-denial. We know there will be a solution, that it will taste like fresh-baked cookies and will simultaneously lower cholesterol, fight osteoporosis, and melt off unwholesome flab. We *know* this. What we have almost forgotten to wonder about is this: since when is breakfast cereal a *moral* issue?

Morality is no longer a prominent feature of civil society. In the 1980s, politicians abandoned it, Wall Street discarded it, televangelists defiled it. Figuratively speaking, we went for the sucrose rush and forgot the challenge of fiber. But only figuratively. For as virtue drained out of our public lives, it reappeared in our cereal bowls, our exercise regimens, and our militant responses to cigarette smoke, strong drink, and greasy food.

We redefined virtue as health. And considering the probable state of our souls, this was not a bad move. By relocating the seat of virtue from the soul to the pecs, the abs, and the coronary arteries, we may not have become the most virtuous people on earth, but we surely became the most desperate for grace. We spend $5 billion a year on our health-club memberships, $2 billion on vitamins, nearly $1 billion on home-exercise equipment, and $6 billion on sneakers to wear out on our treadmills and StairMasters. We rejoice in activities that leave a hangover of muscle pain and in foods that might, in more temperate times, have been classified as fodder. To say we want to be healthy is to gravely understate the case. We want to be *good*.

Consider my own breakfast cereal, a tasteless, colorless substance that clings to the stomach lining with the avidity of Krazy Glue. Quite wisely, the box makes no promise of good taste or visual charm. Even the supposed health benefits are modestly outlined in tiny print. No, the incentive here is of a higher nature. "It is the right thing to do," the manufacturer intones on the back of the box, knowing that, however alluring our temptations to evil, we all want to do the right thing.

The same confusion of the moral and the physical pervades my health club. "Commit to get fit!" is the current slogan, the verb reminding us of the moral tenacity that has become so elusive in our human relationships. In the locker room we sound like the inmates of a miraculously rehabilitative women's prison, always repenting, forever resolving: "I shouldn't have had that doughnut this morning." "I wasn't here for two weeks and now I'm going to pay the price." Ours is a hierarchy of hardness. The soft, the slow, the easily tired rate no compassion, only the coldest of snubs.

Health is almost universally recognized as a *kind* of virtue. At least, most cultures strong enough to leave an ethnographic trace have discouraged forms of behavior that are believed to be unhealthy. Nevertheless, most of us recognize that health is not an accomplishment so much as it is a *potential*. My upper-body musculature, developed largely on Nautilus machines, means that I probably *can* chop wood or unload trucks, not that I ever *will*. Human cultures have valued many things—courage, fertility, craftsmanship, and deadly aim among them—but ours is almost alone in valuing not the deed itself but the mere capacity to perform it.

So what is it that drives us to run, lift, strain, and monitor our metabolisms as if we were really accomplishing something—something pure, that is, and noble? Sociologist Robert Crawford argues that outbreaks of American "healthism" coincide with bouts of middle-class anxiety. It was near the turn of the century, a time of economic turmoil and violent labor struggles, that white-collar Americans embarked on their first 1980s-style health craze. They hiked, rode bikes, lifted weights, and otherwise heeded Teddy Roosevelt's call for "the strenuous life." They filtered their water and fussed about bran (though sweets were heavily favored as a source of energy). On the loonier fringe, they tried "electric belts," vibrating chairs, testicle supporters, "water cures," prolonged mastication, and copious enemas—moralizing all the while about "right living" and "the divine laws of health."

Our own health-and-fitness craze began in another period of economic anxiety—the 1970s, when the economy slid into "stagflation" and a college degree suddenly ceased to guarantee a career above the cab-driving level. In another decade—say the 1930s or the 1960s—we might have mobilized for economic change. But the 1970s was the era of *How to Be Your Own Best Friend* and *Looking Out for Number One*, a time in which it seemed more important, or more feasible, to reform our bodies than to change the world. Bit by bit and with the best of intentions, we began to set aside the public morality of participation and protest for the personal morality of health.

Our fascination with fitness has paid off. Fewer Americans smoke than did fifteen years ago; they drink less hard liquor, eat more fiber and less fat. Our rate of heart disease keeps declining, our life expectancy is on the rise. We are less dependent on doctors, more aware of our own responsibility for health. No doubt we feel better too, at least those of us who have the means and the motivation to give up bourbon for Evian and poker for racquetball. I personally am more confident and probably more durable as a fitness devotee than I ever was in my former life as a chairwarmer.

But there's a difference between health and health*ism*, between health as a reasonable goal and health as a transcendent value. By confusing health and virtue, we've gotten testier, less tolerant, and ultimately less capable of confronting the sources of disease that do *not* lie within our individual control. Victim blaming, for example, is an almost inevitable side effect of healthism. If health is our personal responsibility, the reasoning goes, then disease must be our *fault*.

I think of the friend—a thoroughly intelligent, compassionate, and (need I say?) ultrafit person—who called to tell me that her sister was facing surgery for a uterine tumor. "I can't understand it," my friend confided. "I'm sure she's been working out." *Not quite enough* was the implication, however, despite the absence of even the frailest connection between fibroids and muscle tone. But like pretechnological tribalists, we've come to see every illness as a punishment for past transgressions. When Chicago mayor Harold Washington died of a heart attack almost three years ago, some eulogizers offered baleful mutterings about his penchant for unreformed, high-cholesterol soul food. When we hear of someone getting cancer, we mentally scan their lifestyle for the fatal flaw—fatty foods, smoking, even "repressed anger."

There are whole categories of disease that cannot, in good conscience, be blamed on the lifestyles or moral shortcomings of their victims. An estimated 25,000 cancer deaths a year, for example, result from exposure to the pesticides applied so lavishly in agribusiness. Ten thousand Americans are killed every year in industrial accidents; an estimated 20,000 more die from exposure to carcinogens in the workplace—asbestos, toxic solvents, radiation. These deaths are preventable, but not with any amount of oat bran or low-impact aerobics. Environmental and occupational diseases will require a far more rigorous social and political regimen of citizen action, legislation, and enforcement.

Even unhealthy lifestyles can have "environmental" as well as personal origins. Take the matter of diet and smoking. It's easy for the middle-class fiber enthusiast to look down on the ghetto dweller who smokes cigarettes and spends her food stamps on Doritos and soda pop. But in low-income neighborhoods convenience stores and fast-food joints are often the only sources of food, while billboards and TV commercials are the primary sources of nutritional "information." Motivation is another problem. It's one thing to give up smoking and sucrose when life seems long and promising, quite another when it might well be short and brutal.

Statistically speaking, the joggers and bran eaters are concentrated in the white-collar upper-middle class. Blue- and pink-collar people still tend to prefer Bud to Evian and meat loaf to poached salmon. And they still smoke—at a rate of 51 percent, compared with 35 percent for people in professional and managerial occupations. These facts should excite our concern: Why not special cardiovascular-fitness programs for the assembly-line worker as well as the executive? Reduced-rate health-club memberships for truck drivers and typists? Nutritional supplements for the down-and-out? Instead, healthism tends to reinforce longstanding prejudices. If healthy habits are an expression of moral excellence, then the working class is not only "tacky," ill-mannered, or whatever else we've been encouraged to believe—it's morally deficient.

Thus, perversely, does healthism ease the anxieties of the

affluent. No amount of straining against muscle machines could have saved Drexel Burnham operatives from unemployment; no aerobic exercises can reduce the price of a private-school education. But fitness *can* give its practitioners a sense of superiority over the potbellied masses. On the other side of victim blaming is an odious mood of self-congratulation: "We" may not be any smarter or more secure about our futures. But surely we are more disciplined and pure.

In the end, though—and the end does come—no one is well served by victim blaming. The victim isn't always "someone else," someone fatter, lazier, or more addicted to smoke and grease. The fact is that we do die, all of us, and that almost all of us will encounter disease, disability, and considerable discomfort either in the process or along the way. The final tragedy of healthism is that it leaves us so ill prepared for the inevitable. If we believe that health is a sign of moral purity and anything less is a species of sin, then death condemns us all as failures. Longevity is not a resoundingly interesting lifetime achievement, just as working out is not exactly a life's work.

Somehow, we need to find our way back to being healthy without being health*ist*. Health is great. It makes us bouncier and probably happier. Better yet, it can make us fit *for* something: strong enough to fight the big-time polluters, for example, the corporate waste dumpers; tough enough to take on economic arrangements that condemn so many to poverty and to dangerous occupations; lean and powerful enough to demand a more nurturing, less anxiety-ridden social order.

Health is good. But it is not, as even the ancient and athletic Greeks would have said, *the* good.

[1990]

So's Your Old Lady

So far the debate over high-tech pregnancies for the post-menopausal has centered on the issue of whether a seventy-five-year-old, possibly senile and walker-bound, is a fit guardian for a child who has reached the gun-toting, coke-snorting stage. This is an interesting question to ponder, but the real issue has to do with the mental competency of any woman who would volunteer for pregnancy, especially when she has the reasonable excuse of old age. Are such women feminist heroines, as some of the sisters are arguing? Or are they so deeply disturbed that any resulting offspring should be remanded to foster care at the moment of birth?

Some will say I am indifferent to the sufferings of the elderly infertile population, which craves nothing so much as a few toddlers to brighten up life in the nursing home. But the advocates of late-life parturition know nothing of, or else have mercifully forgotten, the experience of pregnancy itself: the nightmarish symptoms, the ghastly sequelae which can leave a woman disfigured for life. If men had to endure even a fraction of this in the cause of reproduction—the nausea, stretch marks, lethargy, hemorrhoids, varicose veins—you may be sure that the Right-to-Life movement would fold overnight.

Furthermore, and contrary to the impression created by Demi Moore and others in the pregnant pinup line of work, pregnancy has been getting harder, not easier, over time. Two decades ago, when I was making my own contribution to the continuance of the species, pregnancy was considered so simple that even a fifteen-year-old could pull it off. True, there were a few prohibitions—as against bungee jumping and kickboxing in the final months—but generally one was encouraged to treat the whole thing as if it were nothing more than a bout of inexplicable obesity. Doctors warned against the consumption of food, which could lead one's husband to wander, but they actively pushed alcohol, which was known to have a soothing effect on the uterine lining.

Today, however, a medically correct pregnancy resembles a stay in a drug detox ward operated by one of Pol Pot's successors. It is impossible to enter any venue, including an airplane, where alcohol might possibly be imbibed, without encountering signs warning how one little nip could make your baby turn out cross-eyed and pinheaded. Self-respecting women are reduced to carrying a flask disguised as liquid iron supplement in order to survive the endless well-meaning lectures on the teratogenic effects of aspirin and coffee and undercooked meat. As for smoking: you might as well snatch an infant from its carriage and publicly strangle it as reach into your maternity smock and pull out a fag.

The argument is that if doddering old men can have babies, why shouldn't we? But late-life childbearing is an entirely different matter for old geezers compared to old girls. Not only does a man get to skip pregnancy, but the eventual child is genetically related to him. Not so with a fifty-nine-year-old mom, who is forced to carry a child conceived—through some sort of high-tech hanky-panky—by her husband and *another woman.* Imagine being approached by your husband saying, "Uh, my girlfriend and I would like to have a child together, but she's awfully vain about her figure, so we were wondering if, uh . . ."

Then there is the inevitable outcome, so brilliantly portrayed in the movie *Honey, I Blew Up the Kid*. Not long ago, child raising was sufficiently undemanding that it could be left to servants or to women who were otherwise employed full-time at spinning, sheepherding, and the like. Today, however, the whole business has gotten so complicated and psychologically perilous that able-bodied young couples are routinely reduced to cowering wrecks by some seven-foot-tall toddler or furniture-devouring demon child.

But who knows? Perhaps it makes sense to relegate child-bearing to the wearers of adult diapers and elasticized slacks. The young and the sound-minded have other options in life, and there's no reason those nursing homes couldn't double as nursery schools, with the same calm, professional staff tending both baby and mom.

[1994]

A New Boom to Die For

Nothing concentrates the mind like Dr. Jack Kevorkian's gaunt visage on the TV screen as he is led away from yet another assisted-suicide site. Even more riveting, if possible, are the throngs of supporters shown protesting his latest arrest with banners insisting on their right to die swiftly and painlessly. One can only applaud Dr. Jack and his farsighted fans, but still, there is something a wee bit unsettling about the new popularity of death.

Not so long ago, dying was considered an unfortunate business, best left to the neighbors and those loose-living, coked-up celebrities. Death itself was an unmentionable prospect, so that whole generations grew up believing that immortality was the general rule, except for those who bothered to smoke or were reckless enough to eat butter.

But in time anyone could see that the dying enjoy huge advantages compared to the living. Consider the health-care industry, for example, which consigns the living to hospitals, where they are callously tortured and sometimes dismembered—while the dying are allowed into hospices, where they can attend support groups and sing folk songs with nuns.

Perhaps it was inevitable that "dead" should become a desirable status, worth flouting the law to achieve. With hindsight, you could have seen this coming about a decade ago, when the baby-boom generation reached age thirty-five and, suddenly, "middle-aged" ceased to be synonym for "washed up" and became a dashing new sequel to adolescence. If you were tired of the tranquil twenties, you could look forward to the fitful forties, when the famed "mid-life crisis" would be followed ideally by a new career as an aerobics instructor or marriage to a famous sex therapist.

Then the boomers reached age forty-five, and the next phase to be rehabilitated was menopause—a term so menacing it had never before been spoken out loud. Even the hyping of PMS, the disease with a thousand symptoms, had done nothing to improve the image of menopause, which reportedly transformed ripe matrons into crones overnight. But in the fresh genre of menopause books, cronehood became the very pinnacle of the female life cycle. Those still too young for hot flashes were encouraged to fake them—or be dismissed as girls by real women.

Next, as the boomers pushed toward fifty, the period of dotage had to be skillfully recrafted. The American Association of Retired Persons, backed up by the Centrum Silver commercials, began to urge the young to get over their condition as fast as they could and embark on the adventure of senior citizenship. In no time at all, the beautiful people had revived the eighteenth-century fashion of powdering their hair white, and were besieging their plastic surgeons with demands for face-drops and varicosity implants.

Death itself remained a black hole, so to speak, until a number of intrepid people had been there and back. One of the hottest literary topics of the 1990s is the "near-death" experience, which involves wriggling through a dark tunnel and out into the radiant light—where, as it turns out, all one's departed relatives are lined up and waiting. Even so, death is looking more and more attractive, especially to those facing another week in the office. We thought it was a trip to the void, but it turns out to be a growth experience.

Hollywood has pitched in with a whole genre of prodeath productions. Once, only the undead had major roles, as zombies, for example, and ghouls; now they are being elbowed out by the dying and the actually dead. In movies like *Ghost* and *Dying Young* we learned how much more appealing witless young actors become when they sicken and eventually die. In *Fearless* a man is drawn back to his near-death experience, klieg lights and all, while in *My Life* Michael Keaton is delivered from this vale of tears by an inoperable tumor.

But if death is looking good, this may be because the alternative is not what it used to be. Strange, you might say, that in this best of all possible worlds, where almost everyone is free and some are even fed, intelligent people are busily checking the exits.

[1993]

Coming of Age

They were already there when I reached womanhood, these two perpetual big-sister figures of my life—Helen Gurley Brown and Betty Friedan—and here they are again, waiting at the portals of old age. They had good news thirty years ago, as I saw it: You can have sex! Brown announced in *Sex and the Single Girl* (1962). And ambitions, too! Friedan told us in *The Feminine Mystique* (1963). Now, with *The Late Show* (Brown) and *The Fountain of Age* (Friedan), they've been busily clearing the path to the grave, and age, they report, is even better than what came before. An adventure, a fresh realm of achievement and freedom. I should throw in the brilliant, erratic Germaine Greer, who, in *The Change*, finds age to be a journey of spiritual discovery and mystic contentment.

I would like to believe them, even more than I did when I was twenty. There should be some sort of reward for anyone who survives the typical half-century of sticky countertops, family feuds, rejections, heartbreaks, collection agencies, and, finally, hot flashes. General applause whenever one emerges into the street would be fitting, not to mention inner peace or the transcendent insights that visit Greer in her East Anglian garden. But there is an odd thing the preaged can't help but notice: for all the hype about the joys of late life, no one is rushing to enter that exalted state. The words—"I can't wait to look and feel a little older; about seventy would be nice"— have not yet been uttered on this earth.

So it's a pleasant surprise, at first, to see how busy and fulfilled these older women are—catching planes, running enterprises, doing research, hobnobbing with the stars. If this is "old age," the middle-aged may wonder, are we ever going to be in shape for it?

In fact, after a while there gets to be something a little exhausting about the new feminist oeuvre on aging. Friedan and Brown are especially frenetic, each in her own way, of course. Feeling down? Get busy, Brown advises, "busy doing *anything.*" Meditation for example, or shopping, or working out. Friedan is a virtual blur as she moves through the 600-plus pages of *The Fountain of Age*—hiking with the Outward Bound program, attending high-minded seminars at Harvard, deciding whether to study "all the symphonies and the chamber music of Beethoven" or to go cross-country skiing in Yosemite. Even the infinitely more philosophical Greer engenders, at least in this writer, the anxious feeling that the contemplative life isn't worth much unless it culminates in a densely footnoted 400-page tome.

Slow down! I want to call out to them. You've done enough to inspire and instruct whole generations of women. You deserve a break! Helen, get your nose out of your underpants (she lists "smelling your panties" as one of the "small pleasures" of late life) and smell the flowers! Germaine, what is this truculent tone that keeps creeping in, especially when you contemplate Jane Fonda and the estrogen industry? Isn't it time to give anger a rest?

Maybe I just don't trust the old feminist foremoms when it comes to the last phase of life. For one thing, their philosophical approaches are so wildly divergent. Take the simple matter of keeping up one's face: Greer would have us toss our estrogens, liposome creams, and retin-A and face the world haggard and honest. Meanwhile, Brown was getting her face and hands pumped up with silicone until the Food and Drug Administration moved in on this high-risk practice. She quotes Greer, bemusedly, on the futility of late-life cosmetics and then tells us that for her (Brown) "foundation, eye-liner, lip pencil, and blush are almost as fundamental . . . as *teeth*."

Then there's sex. Greer says to give it up and celebrate a manless new life as a "crone." Friedan promises an "intimacy beyond the dreams of youth" as we shed the old gender roles and expectations for a "lovely, naked sharing" unknown to the crass and lustful young. Brown, ever her old kinky, endearing self, would have us keep the vagina in practice by occasionally inserting a greased banana—"and there are papier-mâché bananas out there that *last*."

The problem, I am beginning to think, is that we are being advised to face the end stage in exactly the same spirit we were told, thirty years ago, to stride out into the early summer of life. Be bold! Go for it! Don't take any guff! This is excellent advice, on the face of it, for anyone facing the double burden of being older and female. Thirty years ago, when we were merely female, the expectation was that we would vanish forthwith into the suburbs and supermarkets. Even deeper prejudices await aging women, who are usually portrayed, as on *Golden Girls*, as subsisting on a combination of canasta and gossip. So the first thought is, of course, We'll show *them*!

What is left out is that the fifties and sixties are not just an update of the twenties and thirties. Something different is going on, we can't help notice, as friends and colleagues get picked off by cancer and heart attacks. This is not a phase that ends in marriage or a Nobel prize or promotion to branch manager (though all those things may well happen at any point). This is a phase that ends in death. Like it or not, the great psychic task of the later years is not to be busier, prettier, or more productive than anyone else, but to be prepared to die. And this is one task, the philosophers agree, that cannot be accomplished in a condition of terminal busyness.

Greer at first seems to be the least in denial, the most willing to admit there is something irreversible going on—until we notice how thoroughly she confuses the death of the woman with the death of the womb. Menopause, for her, is already so suffused with "grief" and "mourning" that it is hard to imagine how she will handle the far grimmer changes that may lie ahead. Come now, one wants to say, who needed those periods anyway? As for Friedan and Brown, they see death principally as a goad to further frenzies of achievement. The "only big question," Friedan tells us, "is how are we going *to live* the years we have left . . . What adventures can we now set out on to make sure we'll be alive when we die?"

The fact is that we will be dead when we die—and nothing in our individualistic, competitive souls prepares us to think not just of "death," in the sense of a deadline, but of actually being dead: as in *no more me*. In the Western, capitalistic culture that has triumphed now everywhere, the measure of a life is the self—its pleasures, acquisitions, accomplishments. There is only one paradigm for existence, and it hangs from that lonely little vertical pronoun "I." I dash about, therefore I am. "Not-I" is unthinkable, a terrifyingly smooth, blank wall that stops the imagination in its tracks and leaves it whimpering. In our societywide solipsism, one's own death presents as dark a night as the extinction of a species, the End of Everything.

But surely there is so much more in the world than "I," some of which we should have glimpsed, at least, by the time we reach old age. I am talking not about the mystic oneness Greer reports achieving, admirable as that may be, but about something much more human-scale. For our peasant great-

great-grandmothers, who had little chance to experience the triumphant "I" of modern life, it was the sense of being part of the larger flow of the generations. They lived submerged in the extended family, most of our ancestresses, watching their own decline matched by the rise of grandchildren and great-grandchildren.

Most of us modern, urban-type women don't live immersed in kin. We are childless, like Greer and Brown; or our children have been slow about producing a tribe of grandchildren; or they've moved a continent away. Besides, we've had a lot of other things on our minds in addition to weddings, showers, birthdays, and other markers of biological continuity and flow. We've had our work, for example, our causes and beliefs. We've marched, we've lobbied, we've tried in dozens of ways to make a tiny difference in the world. And somehow, through all these things, we must have sensed some continuity of yearning and effort that extends beyond our individual lives, some community or craft that puts the flickering, unstable "I" in calm perspective. To reach old age without ever believing in something "larger" than oneself which makes life worth living and perhaps worth giving up—well, that would be tragedy unredeemed.

Not that individual death isn't tragic every time, especially to those left behind with only a ghastly, odd-shaped hole in the place where a friend or loved one had once been. Only the fanatic, or the militarist, can imagine that a single human death is truly incidental. But the person who has lived for *something* beyond herself—her political convictions, a special enterprise or craft—always leaves the living with something more constructive to do than weep. I can't bring back my dear friend Andrea, for example, who died of cancer last spring at the age of forty-eight, but I can try to make the things she cared about keep going. In the words of my favorite Holly Near song, "It could have been me, but instead it was you, so I'll keep doing the things you were doing as if I were two."

Feminism is just the kind of cause that ought to temper the injuries of age. To have lived for women's human rights, knowing that they contain a whole new idea of what "human" might become, and then to grow older watching the fresh young faces come along, saying what I might have said, or smarter versions of the same—that is about as close to immortality as I would ever want to be.

So it is sad that our feminist aging books have nothing to say about feminism itself: that it will not age, that it will live on, even after Greer and Brown and Friedan are gone, and thus that they will, in some form, live on, too. Nowhere in these hundreds of pages will you find the simple statement, which any one of these women would be entitled to make:

I've done many interesting and important things in my life, but none so important as helping give other women confidence and power. Now that I'm old [excuse me, Helen, old*er*], I have the boundless satisfaction of seeing new generations of young women and men come along, believing in what I have believed, picking up the torch, carrying on the struggle, and so on and so forth . . .

Ours has been a movement of the daughters, often hostile to the mothers we left behind. Daughters are by their nature full of angry striving, blazing ambition, snarly impatience— which is how they have to be if they intend to make a revolution. But even the most heroic rebel-daughter must grow up, grow old, and let other daughters take her place. Not that we can ever afford to lose the likes of Friedan and Greer and Brown, as their spirited new books remind us. I just want to say thanks, old warrior-women, but the secret of aging is this: that as long as I live, and my daughter after me, so, in some way, will you.

[1993]

SEX

SKIRMISHES

AND

GENDER

WARS

Women Would Have Known

Imagine giving a group of guys that includes Ted (Chappaquiddick, Palm Beach) Kennedy a case of alleged sexual harassment to review. I have the greatest respect for Kennedy's stalwart liberalism and even for a few of his fellows on the Senate Judiciary Committee, but isn't this a little like asking Michael Milken to monitor the SEC? The Senators, after all, occupy a world where women figure less as friends and colleagues than as dangerous, Donna Rice–like characters, capable of decimating a man's career. In the locker rooms of the U.S. Senate, it's the male who is likely to be seen as a "victim" and the female as a wrecker from hell or the enemy party.

Of course, they "didn't get it," as millions of American women screamed in chorus when they found out that the committee had read Anita Hill's charges of sexual harassment against Clarence Thomas months before his confirmation hearings, and tossed them into the circular file. Probably nobody ever asked Joe Biden why a cute little number like him would want a career in politics. Chances are no officemate ever let his or her hand drift languorously over John C. Danforth's derriere or inquired as to Orrin Hatch's vital dimensions.

One can just see them sitting there, when Hill's charges first came to their attention, stroking their chins and clearing their throats. Well, he didn't actually touch her. (Harrumph, harrumph.) She waited all this time. (Shifting in seats.) She seems to have kept in touch with him for years afterward. (Rolling of eyes.) Pretty vague anyway, this sex-harassment business: one woman's "harassment" could be another one's turn-on. (Snickers and elbowings, man to man.)

Well, let's consider what sexual harassment is, starting with the grossest, most obvious case, the kind in which there is both "touching" and an explicit quid pro quo: Do this, and you'll get an A. Come in here with me for a moment, and then we'll talk about that promotion or that bonus or whether you're going to have a job tomorrow. Even a senator, I should think, would see the crime in this. At best, it's sex for pay. At worst, it's a nonviolent variant of rape in which sex is extracted under threat of economic destruction.

But suppose there's no explicit quid pro quo, just a friendly invitation to party. As either of our two female senators could have explained without reference to notes, men and women do not yet meet on what is exactly a level playing field. Nine times out of ten, it's the male who has the power, the female who must flatter, cajole, and make a constant effort to please. If she turns him down, her career may begin to slide. She won't get the best job assignments. He might not be around when she needs help someday—as Hill apparently did—in getting a job or a grant.

Now suppose that the alleged harassment includes no physical touching, no hands-on (at least, let us assume hands) sex. Even with all hands flat on the desk or table, a peculiar kind of sex can be enacted. If our hypothetical harasser should, hypothetically speaking, memorize the screenplays of porno flicks for the delectation of his female underlings, he is in effect asking them to participate in a sexual tableau of his own devising. Some men pay women for the same service or patronize 900 numbers devoted to dirty talk. To have to listen to a man's sexual fantasies is to be forced, at least for the moment, to share them. (With animals? No kidding.) And that is a level of intimacy that even married people, in couples, often choose to forgo for the sake of their mutual illusions.

Finally, suppose there's no touching, no tableau, no quid pro quo—just a crude exploratory gambit along the lines of "Hiya, babe, you wanna . . . ?" Here, too, some moral Rubicon has been crossed. Intimacy in a public setting is not just "inappropriate," in the prissy, yuppie sense. It can be deeply insulting, which is why a misapplied *tu* in French or *du* in German can be a fighting word. When we leave our homes to go to work, we assume an impersonal role like "teacher," "secretary," or "judge." We may even don a special costume (black robes, skirted suit) to get the point across: "This is the public me—not the mommy or the sweetheart or the wife, but the secretary or the judge." To be sexually harassed, even verbally, is to have that robe ripped off and the pearls torn from around your neck. The message of the harasser is, *You're* not a secretary, judge, whatever. Not to me you aren't. To me, you're a four-letter word that family magazines refuse to print.

There's hardly a woman alive who doesn't know how it feels to have her dignity punctured, her public role ripped away, by some fellow with a twinge in his groin. You feel naked. You feel that you (yes, you) have made some ghastly mistake, sent the wrong signals, led him along. At first you try to pretend it didn't happen. You may do what I once did and keep lifting his hand off your knee as if it were some object that happened to fall there. You may even maintain the fiction of friendship for years, because anything is better than being demoted, in your own mind, to a deletable four-letter word.

Given the views of Judge Thomas and his supporters, it is

a glorious irony that his confirmation process provided such a powerful argument for affirmative action, starting in the U.S. Senate. Fourteen guys *could* have seen sexual harassment as a charge worth following up on from the moment it crossed their desks. At least there is no anatomical defect that prevents the male brain from thinking the thought: "Sexual harassment is a serious offense. Sexual harassment by the one man responsible for investigating cases of sexual harassment would be worse than a serious offense—it would be proof of a brazen contempt for the law."

But they didn't think that. They thought "big deal," or some fancy legal version thereof. And there could be no better proof of the need to start populating positions of power with people of more than one sex. On some subjects, for reasons both historic and tragic, women know best.

[1991]

Feminism

Confronts Bobbittry

To read the volumes of outraged male commentary, you'd think Lorena Bobbitt had got her training in a feminist guerrilla camp and her carving skills from the SCUM (Society for Cutting Up Men) Manifesto. "Go out into the world," her trainers must have told her, "find some sexist lowlife, preferably an ex-Marine named John Wayne, and, you know, cut it off!"

But Lorena Bobbitt is in many ways just your typical small-town multicultural manicurist, a woman whose ideas of political science are summed up in a statement she made about Venezuela, where she grew up: "I have a patriotism . . . We do have McDonald's. We do have Pizza Hut." Nor are the women who harassed Dr. James Sehn's wife in a McLean, Virginia, beauty parlor because he had helped reattach the offending organ known to be commandos from the National Organization for Women. In fact, the really interesting thing about the Bobbitt affair is the huge divergence it reveals between high-powered feminist intellectualdom, on the one hand, and your average office wit or female cafeteria orator, on the other.

While the gals in data entry are discussing fascinating new possibilities for cutlery commercials, the feminist pundits are tripping over one another to show that none of them is, goddess forbid, a "man hater." And while the pundits are making obvious but prissy-sounding statements like "The fact that one has been a victim doesn't give one carte blanche to victimize others," the woman in the street is making V signs by raising two fingers and bringing them together with a snipping motion.

If the feminist intellectuals seem slightly out of touch, it's because they're preoccupied these days with their own factional matters, such as the great standoff over the subject of victimhood. On the provictimhood side are the legions of domestic-abuse specialists who see Lorena Bobbitt as one more martyr in women's long, weepy history of rape and abuse. On the anti side are feminist authors like Naomi Wolf, who claim that women have been turning away from feminism because they're sick and tired of hearing about victims and "victimology": foot binding, battering, genital mutilation, witch burnings, and the like. Time to stop whining, the antivictimhood feminists say, and go for the power.

Both sides make valid points. It's just that neither seems to grasp the brazen new mood out there represented by, among other things, all the grassroots female backing for Ms. Bobbitt. The retail clerks who send her letters of support, the homemakers who cackle wildly every time they sharpen the butcher knife are neither "tired of hearing about victims" nor eager to honor them. They're tired of *being* victims. And they're eager to see women fight back by whatever means necessary.

Probably it all started when Louise—or was it Thelma?— dispatched that scumball would-be rapist in the parking lot of a bar. In fact, we can't get enough of warrior-woman flicks: Sigourney Weaver in *Alien*, Linda Hamilton in *Terminator II*, Sharon Stone in *Basic Instinct*. These are ladies who wouldn't slice anything off, one suspected, unless they meant to put it straight into a Cuisinart.

In the real world, the new mood was manifested by all the

women flocking to gun stores and subscribing to Women & Guns, the magazine that tells you how to accessorize a neat little sidearm. And, without any prompting from NOW, thousands of women are sporting bumper stickers identifying themselves as BEYOND BITCH and buying T-shirts that say TOUGH ENOUGH or make unflattering comparisons between cucumbers and human males.

The new grassroots female militancy is not something that a women's studies professor would judge p.c. In fact, it looks a lot like your standard conservative anticrime backlash, but with a key difference: crime in this case is defined as what men have been getting away with for centuries.

Organized feminism, of course, had a lot to do with the emergence of the new beyond-bitch attitude. Feminism raised expectations, giving millions of women the idea that makeup is not the solution to chronic bruising and that even males may be endowed with coffee-making skills. But for most women, especially the kind who don't do book tours and talk shows, the feminist revolution just hasn't come along fast enough. A sizable percentage of them have to work every day with guys whose notions of gender etiquette are derived from Howard Stern and Rush Limbaugh. And all too many women go home to Bobbitt-like fellows who regard the penis as a portable battering ram.

So the ripple of glee that passed through the female population when Lorena Bobbitt struck back shows that feminist intellectualdom has it wrong. In polls, American women are strongly supportive of feminist issues, and if they nonetheless shrink from the *F* word itself, this is not because they think it means man-hating militants from hell. On the contrary, the problem with "feminism" may be that it has come to sound just too damn dainty.

Personally, I'm for both feminism and nonviolence. I admire the male body and prefer to find the penis attached to it rather than having to root around in vacant lots with Ziploc bag in hand. But I'm not willing to wait another decade or two for gender peace to prevail. And if a fellow insists on using his penis as a weapon, I say that, one way or another, he ought to be swiftly disarmed.

[1994]

Sorry, Sisters, This Is Not the Revolution

American feminism late-1980s-style could be defined, cynically, as women's rush to do the same foolish and benighted things that have traditionally occupied men. And why not? The good and honest things that have traditionally occupied women—like rearing children and keeping husbands in clean shirts—are valued in the open market at somewhere near the minimum wage. And whatever one thinks of investment banking or corporate law, the perks and the pay are way ahead of those for waitressing and data entry. So every time a woman breaks a new barrier, the rest of us tend to cheer—even if she's running a pollution-producing company or toting a gun in some ill-considered war.

Two cheers, anyway. Because this is not the revolution that I, at least, signed on for. When the feminist movement burst forth a couple of decades ago, the goal was not just to join 'em—and certainly not just to beat 'em—but to improve an imperfect world. Gloria Steinem sketched out the vision in a 1970 essay titled "What It Would Be Like If Women Win." What it would be like was a whole lot better, for men as well as women, because, as she said right up front, "Women don't want to exchange places with men." We wanted *better* places, in a kinder, gentler, less rigidly gendered world.

We didn't claim that women were morally superior. But they had been at the receiving end of prejudice long enough, we thought, to empathize with the underdog of either sex. Then, too, the values implicit in motherhood were bound to clash with the "male values" of competitiveness and devil-may-care profiteering. We imagined women storming male strongholds and, once inside, becoming change agents, role models, whistle-blowers. The hand that rocks the cradle was sure to rock the boat.

To a certain extent, women have "won." In medicine, law, and management, they have increased their participation by 300 percent to 400 percent since the early 1970s, and no one can argue that they haven't made *some* difference. Women lawyers have spearheaded reforms in the treatment of female victims of rape and of battering. Women executives have created supportive networks to help other women up the ladder and are striving to sensitize corporations to the need for flexible hours, child care, and parental leave. Women journalists have fought to get women's concerns out of the "style section" and onto the front page. Women doctors, according to physician-writer Perri Klass, are less paternalistic than their male counterparts and "better at listening."

But, I'm sorry, sisters, this is not the revolution. What's striking, from an old-fashioned (circa 1970) feminist perspective, is just how *little* has changed. The fact that law is no longer classified as a "nontraditional" occupation for women has not made our culture any less graspingly litigious or any more concerned with the rights of the underdog. Women doctors haven't made a dent in the high-tech, bottom-line fixation of the medical profession, and no one would claim that the influx of executive women has ushered in a new era of high-toned business ethics.

It's not that we were wrong back in the salad days of feminism about the existence of nurturant "feminine values." If anything, women have more distinctive views as a sex than they did twenty years ago. The gender gap first appeared in the presidential election of 1980, with women voting on the more liberal side. Recent polls show that women are more likely to favor social spending for the poor and to believe it's "very important" to work "for the betterment of American society."

So why haven't our women pioneers made more of a mark? Charitably speaking, it may be too soon to expect vast transformations. For one thing, women in elite, fast-track positions are still pathetically scarce. *Fortune* magazine reported in July 1990 that fewer than one-half of one percent of top-echelon corporate managers are female. Then there's the exhaustion factor. Women are far more likely to work a "double day" of career plus homemaking. The hand that rocks the cradle—and cradles the phone, and sweeps the floor, and writes the memo, and meets the deadline—doesn't have time to reach out and save the world.

But I fear, too, that women may be losing the idealistic vision that helped inspire feminism in the first place. Granted, every Out group—whether defined by race, ethnicity, or sexual preference—seeks assimilation as a first priority. But every Out group carries with it a critical perspective, forged in the painful experiences of rejection and marginalization. When that perspective is lost or forgotten, a movement stands in danger of degenerating into a scramble for personal advancement. We applaud the winners and pray that their numbers increase, but the majority will still be found far outside the gates of privilege, waiting for the movement to start up again.

And for all the pioneering that brave and ambitious women have done, the female majority remains outside, earning seventy cents to the man's one dollar in stereotypically female jobs. That female majority must still find a way to survive the uncaring institutions, the exploitative employers, and the deep social inequities the successful few have not yet got around to challenging.

Maybe, now that women have got a foot in the door, it's time to pause and figure out what we intend to do when we get inside. Equality with men is a fine ambition, and I'll fight for any woman's right to do any foolish or benighted thing that men are paid and honored for. But, ultimately, assimilation is just not good enough. As one vintage feminist T-shirt used to say, IF YOU THINK EQUALITY IS THE GOAL . . . YOUR STANDARDS ARE TOO LOW.

[1990]

What Do Women

Have to Celebrate?

Maybe plumbing, not biology, is destiny. More than seventy years after women won the vote, the U.S. Senate still has no women's bathroom. Even the Democratic cloakroom in the House has no women's room, leaving female representatives with a hike to the Democratic Women's Reading Room, where there are all of three toilets. Future archaeologists, studying the pipes and bathroom fixtures of Capitol Hill, may conclude that late-twentieth-century America was a fortress of patriarchy on a par with Saudi Arabia.

They would have it wrong, of course. Measured in terms of the number of feminist organizations, journals, support groups, and T-shirts per capita, the United States is the world headquarters of the international feminist conspiracy. The paradox is that all this grassroots energy and commitment has never translated into hard political power: in 1992, the "Year of the Woman," 3 percent of the Senate and 6 percent of the House of Representatives are female—proportions which lag embarrassingly behind most Western European nations.

Which is why the fuss over the Year of the Woman always sounded a little menacing—a way of saying, "This is your chance, gals. Now or never."

But 1992 will deserve a place in "her-story" as the year women stormed the Hill. One hundred seventeen women ran for seats in the House and Senate, way ahead of the previous record—seventy-seven in 1990. In another first, twenty-one of the female challengers were women of color, up from fourteen in 1990.

The Year of the Woman must have come as a surprise to the many who have written feminism's obituary over the years. In the 1980s feminism was supposed to have been supplanted by mild-mannered, skirted-suited "postfeminists" who wanted nothing more than a reliable babysitter and a chance to bang their heads against the corporate glass ceiling.

But at some point in the last twelve months, a generation of women woke up to the possibility that what they had taken for granted could also be taken away. As the Supreme Court began to nibble away at *Roe v. Wade*, "choice" took on the moral urgency that in another generation had been reserved for Vietnam. And then came "Hill-Thomas." It was the visual that lingered long after the testimony, and the visual showed fourteen white men confronting a species of human being that they would normally encounter only in the form of a hotel maid. Little "clicks" of raised consciousness could be heard throughout the land as women plotted to integrate the Senate Judiciary Committee.

So it was goodbye, postfeminism; hello, third wave. (The first wave was the suffrage movement, and the second wave began in the 1960s.) The other side of all the neatly tailored women running for office was a far larger number of women running in the streets. In New York, feminists formed the Women's Action Coalition (WAC), a militant direct-action group modeled on the boisterous gay group, ACT UP. During the Democratic Convention, while the female candidates preened and paraded inside, thousands of other women faced down prolife demonstrators at abortion clinics, rallied against violence against women, and published the sassy, hot-pink *Getting It Gazette.*

And there were achievements, as well as adrenaline, to build on. Almost all the women candidates, including Patty ("Just a Mom in Tennis Shoes") Murray from Washington state, had already served in a state legislature. What they needed for the big leap was money, and this had been quietly building up through the 1980s, as a generation of female fast-trackers made partner, moved into corner offices, and got ready to write their own checks. After Hill-Thomas, they couldn't seem to write them fast enough. The bipartisan National Women's Political Caucus raised $61,000 from a single newspaper ad featuring a fantasy scene of Clarence Thomas being grilled by a panel of female senators. EMILY's List, the prochoice Democratic women's donor network, saw its contributions quadruple to an estimated $6 million, making it the largest donor to congressional campaigns in the country.

Still, it might not have been the Year of the Woman if it wasn't also the Year of the Vanishing Man. After a series of scandals left Congress looking like a holding pen for unindicted criminals, the men began to flee as fast as they could get their résumés updated: fifty-three representatives retired or just declined to run again. Others, like New York's Stephen Solarz, found the ground shifting beneath their feet as redistricting removed their comfortable old constituencies. One way or another, a vast empty space opened up, and that great sucking sound, as Ross Perot might have put it, was women rushing in to fill the vacuum.

Well, not every kind of woman. "It's the year of the feminist woman," antifeminist leader Phyllis Schlafly observed tartly. Or at least of the liberal Democratic woman, which is why George Bush was heard to mutter, during the second presidential debate, "I hope a lot of them lose." Of the eleven women who ran for the Senate, ten were Democrats, as were seventy of the 106 female candidates for Congress.

But where else was a woman to go with her tote bag full of "women's issues" if not to the Democratic Party? The Republican Party has "family values," meaning opposition to abortion and gay rights. The Democratic Party has "family issues," meaning things like health care, education, and family leave. It probably helps that Clinton and Gore represent the first generation of presidential candidates to have shared their law school classes with women and their homes with actual feminists. This puts them in a different geological era from Bush, who, when questioned about appointing women to office, mentioned the woman in his administration who's responsible for doling out souvenir tie clips, or from Perot, who cited his wife and "four beautiful daughters."

And in 1992, the year of anti-incumbent fever, female candidates had an appeal that went beyond gender loyalty. Where women voters read "role model," males read "outsider." There was a general expectation that women would be more ethical, less taken by perks and pomp, and more likely to view things from the supermarket-counter level. This, in fact, had been the suffragists' dream: that women would use their innate "mother sense" to bring sweetness and light to the smoke-filled backrooms.

For one brief, defining moment in the middle of the summer, the politics of the nation seemed to have become the politics of gender. On the Republican side, there was a platform borrowed from *The Handmaid's Tale* and Marilyn Quayle to represent the vanishing female option of career wife. Quayle made it clear just how much was at stake when she used her convention speech to go after the Democrats not only for their candidate's draft evasion but for the sexual revolution. This was all-out culture war, baby-boom-style: feminism vs.

antifeminism, repression vs. permission, mixing things up vs. shoring up the walls. Armageddon, in other words, with a female cast.

Strangely, after all the buildup, the moment didn't last. By September, it began to look as though the Year of the Woman would be only eight months long. With national attention focused on the presidential candidates, politics resumed the ancient rhythms of the horse race and the cockfight. "Women's issues," such as domestic violence, never came up in the presidential campaign, and when abortion did intrude into the vice-presidential debate, James Stockdale undercut his own prochoice statement with a grumpy plea to "get past this and talk about something substantive."

Meanwhile, women's campaigns began to sputter and gasp. Despite the success of feminist fund-raisers, most women still occupy a socioeconomic stratum where a $100-a-plate luncheon counts as a new blazer or dental visit forgone. In Kansas, Democratic challenger Gloria O'Dell raised barely $100,000 compared to incumbent Bob Dole's $2 million. California's Barbara Boxer and Pennsylvania's Lynn Yeakel found themselves too broke to counter their opponents' attack ads until late in their campaigns.

Then there was the gradual realization that women do not necessarily inhabit a loftier moral plane than the men they intend to dislodge. Illinois's Carol Moseley Braun got hit by Medicaid-fraud charges for failing to report a family windfall that she might have used to help pay her mother's nursing-home bill. Yeakel was revealed to have paid up $17,000 in back taxes on the eve of announcing her candidacy. Congresswoman Barbara Boxer had 143 bounced checks to account for. In the nastiest race of all, two New York feminists, Geraldine Ferraro and Elizabeth Holtzman, went down biting and clawing—to make way for a liberal man. And, of course, not all the new female candidates were even feminists: Republican challengers Charlene Haar (South Dakota) and Linda Bean (Maine) proudly claimed to be "prolife and progun."

Maybe that's how it should be: pit-bull women, right-wing women, feminist women—all kinds of women in all their glorious diversity. Nothing in our genes, after all, says we have to be kinder, gentler, and more committed to family leave. But with women's representation in national politics still hovering near presuffrage levels, it was only natural that most of the new female candidates would define themselves as feminists and women on a mission. Trailblazing is not a job for the uncommitted.

The winners shouldn't expect to usher in the feminist millennium. With a Clinton administration, there may be some easy wins on the Freedom of Choice Act, family leave, and fetal-tissue research. But in a rating of his program by the Institute for Women's Policy Research in Washington, Clinton received only a B-minus (Bush got a D), and, after a close race, Clinton may be tempted to distance himself from his party's more feminist and liberal wing. In the House and Senate, where women have been traditionally relegated to inconsequential committees, the new crop of freshwomen will be starting at the bottom, struggling to get a word in edgewise. And of course, there'll still be that long, long walk to the women's room.

As for the losers, plus all the women who felt they were too poor, too inexperienced, or too young to run this time: everything that the new female senators and congresswomen manage to accomplish will add to the credibility of the next wave of female candidates. And everything they don't get done will only add to the anger, and hence to the feminist resources, available to fuel the fire next time.

[1992]

Making Sense

of la différence

Few areas of science are as littered with intellectual rubbish as the study of innate mental differences between the sexes. In the nineteenth century, biologists held that woman's brain was too small for intellect, but just large enough for household chores. When the tiny-brain theory bit the dust (elephants, after all, have bigger brains than men), scientists began a long, fruitless attempt to locate the biological basis of male superiority in various brain lobes and chromosomes. By the 1960s sociobiologists were asserting that natural selection, operating throughout the long human prehistory of hunting and gathering, had predisposed males to leadership and exploration and females to crouching around the campfire with the kids.

Recent studies suggest that there may be some real differences after all. And why not? We have different hormones and body parts; it would be odd if our brains were a hundred percent unisex. The question, as ever, is, What do these differences augur for our social roles?—meaning, in particular, the division of power and opportunity between the sexes.

Don't look to the Flintstones for an answer. However human beings whiled away their first 100,000 or so years of existence, few of us today make a living by tracking down mammoths or digging up tasty roots. In fact, much of our genetic legacy of sex differences has already been rendered moot by that uniquely human invention: technology. Military prowess no longer depends on superior musculature or those bursts of aggressive fury that prime the body for combat at ax range. As for exploration, women—with their lower body weight and oxygen consumption—may be the more "natural" astronauts.

But suppose that the feminists' worst-case scenario turns out to be true, and that males really are better, on average, at certain mathematical tasks. If this tempts you to shunt the girls all back to Home Ec—the only acceptable realm for would-be female scientists eighty years ago—you probably need remedial work in the statistics of "averages" yourself. Just as some women are taller and stronger than some men, some are swifter at solid geometry and abstract algebra. Many of the pioneers in the field of X-ray crystallography—which involves three-dimensional visualization and heavy doses of math—were female, including biophysicist Rosalyn Franklin, whose work was indispensable to the discovery of the double-helical structure of DNA.

Then there is the problem that haunts all studies of "innate" sex differences: the possibility that the observed differences are really the result of lingering cultural factors—pushing females, for example, to "succeed" by dummying up. Girls' academic achievement, for example, usually takes a nosedive at puberty. Unless nature has selected for smart girls and dumb women, something is going very wrong at about the middle-school level. Part of the problem may be that males, having been the dominant sex for a few millennia, still tend to prefer females who make them feel stronger and smarter. Any girl who is bright enough to solve a quadratic equation is also smart enough to bat her eyelashes and pretend that she can't.

Teachers too may play a larger role than nature in differentiating the sexes. Studies show that they tend to favor boys by calling on them more often, making eye contact with them more frequently, and pushing them harder to perform. Myra and David Sadker, professors of education at American University, have found that girls do better when teachers are sensitized to gender bias and refrain from sexist language such as the use of "man" to mean all of us. Single-sex classes in math and science also boost female performance, presumably by eliminating favoritism and male disapproval of female achievement.

The success, so far, of such simple educational reforms only underscores the basic social issue: given that there may be real innate mental differences between the sexes, what are we going to do about them? A female advantage in reading emotions could be interpreted to mean that males should be barred from psychiatry—or that they need more coaching. A male advantage in math could be used to confine girls to essays and sonnets—or the decision could be made to compensate by putting more effort into girls' math education. In effect, we already compensate for boys' apparent handicap in verbal skills by making reading the centerpiece of grade-school education.

We are cultural animals, and these are cultural decisions of the kind that our genes can't make for us. In fact, the whole discussion of innate sex differences is itself heavily shaped by cultural factors. Why, for example, is the study of innate differences such a sexy, well-funded topic right now, which happens to be a time of organized feminist challenge to the ancient sexual division of power? Why do the media tend to get excited when scientists find an area of difference, and ignore the many reputable studies that come up with no differences at all?

Whatever science eventually defines it as, *la différence* can be amplified or minimized by human cultural arrangements: the choice is up to us, not our genes.

[1992]

Kiss Me, I'm Gay

A strange, unspoken assumption about human sexuality runs through the current debate on gay rights. Both sides agree, without saying so explicitly, that the human race consists of two types of people: heterosexuals and—on the other side of a great sexual dividing line—homosexuals. Heterosexuals are assumed to be the majority, while gays are thought to be a "minority," analogous to African Americans, Latinos, or any other ethnic group. Thus there is "gay pride" just as there is "black pride." We have Gay Pride marches just as we have Saint Patrick's Day or Puerto Rican Day parades. Gay militants even rallied, briefly, around the idea of a "queer nation."

There are ways in which this tribalistic view of human sexuality is useful and even progressive. Before the gay rights movement, homosexuality was conceived as a diffuse menace, attached to no particular group and potentially threatening every man, at least in its "latent" form. So, naturally, as gays came out, they insisted on a unique and prideful group identity: We're queer and we're here! How else do you get ahead in America except by banding together and hoisting a flag?

Some studies seem to indicate that homosexuality is genetically based, more or less like left-handedness or being Irish.

Heterosexuals, whether out of tolerance or spite, have been only too happy to concede to gays a special and probably congenital identity of their own. It's a way of saying: We're on this side of the great sexual divide—and you're on that.

There's only one problem with the theory of gays-as-ethnic-group: it denies the true plasticity of human sexuality and, in so doing, helps heterosexuals evade that which they really fear. And what heterosexuals really fear is not that "they"—an alien subgroup with perverse tastes in bedfellows—are getting an undue share of power and attention but that "they" might well be us.

Yes, certainly there are people who have always felt themselves to be gay—or straight—since the first unruly fifth-grade crush or tickle in the groin. But for every study suggesting that homosexuality is innate, there are plenty of others that suggest human sexuality is far more versatile—or capricious, if you like. In his pioneering study, Alfred Kinsey reported that 37 percent of the men and 19 percent of the women he surveyed acknowledged having had at least one orgasm with a partner of the same sex. William Masters and Virginia Johnson found that, among the people they studied, fantasies about sex with same-sex partners were the norm.

In some cultures, it is more or less accepted that "straight" men will nonetheless have sex with other men. The rapid spread of AIDS in Brazil, for example, is attributed to bisexual behavior on the part of ostensibly heterosexual males. In the British upper class, homosexual experience used to be a not uncommon feature of male adolescence. Young Robert Graves went off to World War I pining desperately for his schoolboy lover, but returned and eventually married. And, no, he did not spend his time in the trenches buggering his comrades-in-arms.

So being gay is not quite the same as being Irish. There are shadings; there are changes in the course of a lifetime. I know people who were once brazenly "out" and are now happily, heterosexually married—as well as people who have gone in the opposite direction. Or, to generalize beyond genital sexuality to the realm of affection and loyalty: we all know men who are militantly straight yet who reserve their deepest feelings for the male-bonded group—the team, the volunteer fire department, the men they went to war with.

The problem for the military is not that discipline will be undermined by a sudden influx of stereotypically swishy gays. The problem is that the military is still a largely unisexual institution—with all that that implies about the possibility of homosexual encounters. The traditionalists keep bringing up the "crowded showers," much like the dread unisex toilets of the ERA debate. But, from somewhere deep in the sexual imagination, the question inevitably arises: Why do they have such tiny, crowded showers anyway?

By saying that gays are a definite, distinguishable minority that can easily be excluded, the military may feel better about its own presumptive heterosexuality. But can "gays" really be excluded? Do eighteen-year-old recruits really have a firm idea what their sexuality is? The military could deal with its sexuality crisis much more simply, and justly, by ceasing to be such a unisexual institution and letting women in on an equal basis.

Perhaps we have all, "gays" and "straights," gotten as far as we can with the metaphor of gays as a quasi-ethnic group, entitled to its own "rights." Perhaps it is time to acknowledge that the potential to fall in love with, or just be attracted to, a person of the same sex is widespread among otherwise perfectly conventional people. There would still be enormous struggle over what is right and wrong, "normal" and "abnormal." But at least this would be a struggle that everyone—gay or straight—would have a stake in: gays because of who they are; straights because of who they might be, and sometimes actually are. All men, for example, would surely be better off in a world where simple acts of affection between men occasioned no great commentary or suspicion. Where a hug would be a hug and not a "statement."

[1993]

IN THE

REALM

OF THE

SPECTACLE

The Decline

of the Universe

The media moguls are as one in denying that they arranged for the bombardment of Jupiter to coincide with the twenty-fifth anniversary of the first moon walk. "Even Rupert Murdoch cannot wreck a planet just to boost ratings," a spokesman has reportedly said, "certainly not one of your larger-size planets anyway." But who could blame him even if he had personally assembled the comet Shoemaker-Levy 9 and fired it into the backside of Jupiter? It's hard to make the universe interesting these days—just ask the guys at CNN.

Oh, there were a few moments of joy during the brief spasm of media space coverage: the astronomers, for example, whooping and uncorking champagne when they discovered that Jupiter was indeed being significantly scarred. One can only imagine the revelry that would break out in their ranks if something really stupendous had happened—a supernova of the sun, or, perhaps, the moon deciding to revisit its birthplace in what is now the Pacific Ocean.

But for the rest of us, the mood was one of "melancholy" and "a dispiriting sense of unfulfilled promise," as *The New York Times* so eloquently put it. Only twenty-five years ago, we expected great things from the universe. There would be precious metals in abundance, Sigourney Weaver wrestling multimouthed space-creeps, maybe darling gremlinlike E.T.'s who would know the secret of weight loss and agree to become our gurus. But, alas, there was nothing—cubic light-years of nothing, in fact, interrupted by the occasional unoccupied rock.

CNN did its best to hold our interest. Space gives us things, we were told—the hand-held calculator, the cellular phone, not to mention powdered orange juice and freeze-dried chicken à la king. Without space, we would be unable to make phone calls without being bound, by a cord, to the wall; orange juice would have to be extracted from a fruit. But space is not just a grab bag of clever inventions. Space can kill, we were solemnly reminded. If Shoemaker-Levy 9 had decided to touch down on Washington, D.C., instead of Nowheresville, Jupiter—well, imagine the ratings for that. Instead, we were forced to watch a succession of white guys reminisce about how much they had admired space years ago, when their crew cuts were still youthfully brown.

A few channels away there was livelier fare. One of our fine Christian news programs was upstaging mere secular space coverage with some extraterrestrial insights from the Bible. It seems that the book of Ezekiel mentions a "flying scroll," which could not have been your ordinary flying scroll— hurled, say, from a fifth-floor window by an offended reader of scrolls. No, indeed, because Ezekiel gives the exact dimensions of this airborne scroll, and they are, incredibly enough, the dimensions of a flying saucer! If the space guys could get here on their own in those days, when there was nothing but scrolls to ride on, then why should we struggle to get off the planet? The space guys will come back here when they want to, probably in ships resembling videocassettes.

Back on CNN, the mood was slipping from "melancholy" to the black giddiness of despair. "Will mankind ever explore the far reaches of space," the voice-over intoned, "or will we be content to experience the universe in a virtual-reality machine?" Our true destiny, in other words, might not be to conquer space but to be the first cosmic couch potatoes. We will ski the mountains of Ganymede and snorkel the canals of Mars—all without clumsy space suits or having to go outdoors.

Perhaps we will have to settle for the virtual universe anyway. Tragically, space exploration may soon be blocked by the huge amount of man-made debris now orbiting the earth. It could be argued that this debris was necessary and worthwhile, since much of it was created in the course of launching the satellites that now bring us news of O.J.'s prison exercise regimen and Ezekiel's encounters with spaceships. But it may also be that there are some species which are so terminally silly that they deserve to be confined to their planets.

[1994]

Prewatched TV

Everything else has been automated, so why not that most commonplace of human activities—watching TV? This is the true secret of *Beavis and Butt-Head*'s megasuccess: not that they satisfy a young person's normal interest in arson and the torture of small animals and elderly people—which they do, of course, as has often been noted—but that they take the last bit of effort out of watching TV. For anyone so culturally impaired as not yet to have seen it, their show consists largely of two cartoon figures watching TV on a screen which fills up one's own. *They* make the ironic comments; *they* change the channel whenever a video threatens to drag. Hence the little pimple-butts' great gift to humankind—prewatched TV.

They're beginning to make prewatched commercials, too. Just as one's index finger moves to ward off the oncoming "message"—"Zap!"—the channel appears to change to something more entertaining. Then another virtual zap, and the product, whatever it is, returns. This is automated channel surfing—TV-viewing minus the last little vestige of muscular exertion.

At first we loved channel surfing on our own, accessing the collective mind, as it were, by tapping the buttons on the remote. People took pride in their craftsmanship—splicing scenes of hyena predation from the Discovery Channel in with the president's State of the Union address, for example, or alleviating the gloom of Bosnia with nacho recipes from the nearby Food Channel. Creative viewers mixed Hillary on health care with Tonya on skates, or cut into their favorite televangelist with the human sacrifice scene from *The Temple of Doom*. It was all there at one's fingertips: sprightly political chatter, singing transvestites, warnings about Satan, instructions for making béchamel sauce or rehabilitating a codependent relationship.

But then we went into overload. In my neighborhood, the breaking point came when the cable TV company upgraded us from forty to sixty channels, which meant there would now be not only twenty-four-hour news channels but channels offering continuous weather, shopping-by-phone, and trials of celebrity felons. The first casualty was a neighbor who developed a Repetitive Stress Injury by overusing his remote. Now both of his index fingers are in finger-sized casts, and he has been reduced to changing channels with his nose.

Plus it must be acknowledged that channel surfing was one of the factors undermining the American family. Once, it had been a simple matter to settle on the evening's entertainment—sex or violence, X-rated or R. After a brief, usually bloodless tussle, the victors settled down to enjoy and the losers resigned themselves to making irritating comments and exotic eructations, much as Beavis and Butthead now do for us. But when viewing became surfing, the fights got nastier. Children demanded their own TVs, often at gunpoint; spouses dueled with matching his-and-hers remotes. One theory has it that Lorena Bobbitt only went for the penis because the index finger, grossly thickened through overuse, resisted the knife.

Channel surfing has been destroying the nation as well. What, after all, are the fissures that really divide us? White vs. black, right vs. left, or some such archaic dispute? No, of course not. The real divisions are between those who watch MTV and those who favor Christian broadcasting, between CNN viewers and fans of Fox Network. But why let these transitory preferences come between us? American culture is not one or the other—Christian programming or writhing pelvises, "hard" news or Michael Jackson. American culture is everything running in together—béchamel sauce mixed with the Red Hot Chili Peppers, Pat Robertson a microsecond away from Ru Paul.

Some say we should throw our remotes into the recycling bin and go back to the old days, when changing a channel involved walking from couch to set, twisting a knob, and returning, on foot, to couch. But the national attention span has gotten much too short for such arduous interruptions. It's far better to have the channel switching done for us, by some godlike RSI-immune invisible hand. Families, communities, nations will draw closer together as we all watch, i.e., rewatch, the same even-handed, prewatched blur.

[1994]

Blood on the Temple Steps

"It's Economy night!" squeals the local tabloid. CNN brings out a special Economy logo depicting the Capitol building enveloped in layers of fluttering gauze. For more than a week now we have been in countdown mode: so many days to the prespeech, so many days to the real speech—with nobody questioning why there should be one speech to test the waters and another to say "I was only kidding." But who cares? There hasn't been so much excitement since Desert Storm.

In the prespeech, Clinton attempts to mobilize the deep, primitive instincts normally tapped only by Republicans and advertisements for personal grooming products. "Sacrifice," we hear over and over, usually accompanied by "pain" or even, titillatingly, "raw pain." Images of the Aztec empire in its glory days arise, unbidden, in the mind: long lines of youths and maidens having their hearts ripped out to appease some querulous god—in our case, the Economy. When Clinton tells us that patriotism itself demands this sacrifice, a delicious shiver runs through the body politic. It's the Gulf War all over again, with the blood of innocents pouring down the temple steps.

But the day after the prespeech, it is clear that Clinton has gone too far and plunged the nation into a febrile, agitated state. Wall Street sputters. Anonymous men in the street are interviewed, saying things like, "Well, Ah'm willin' to sacrifice if the G'mint is too." Suddenly it appears that the appetite for sacrifice, once awakened, could demand no less than the president himself. Cadres of speech writers tear their hair, shred the prespeech, and begin to work on the respeech. The White House announces that, on the advice of leading psychologists, the hot word "sacrifice" will henceforth be replaced by the calming word "contribution."

Camera crews are dispatched to locales long since thought to have been abandoned by intelligent life, where bankers and car salesmen opine about the need to do something, anything, to "control the deficit." The tone of these remarks indicates that we are, once again, on mythic terrain. What is the Economy, after all? An obese, capricious god, we are encouraged to believe, which cavorted through the 1980s on cocaine and crème fraîche, but is sulking now, due to the Deficit, which has attached itself like a succubus to the Economy's neck. Does the Deficit really matter? What is the Economy, anyway, and what are its intentions and goals? As in the case of the Judeo-Christian deity, these questions remain wrapped in profoundest mystery.

In the media, the only allowable issues are of a gladiatorial nature: will Clinton tackle the deficit or be distracted by hunger and misery? We are reminded that he is being asked to do a trick that has never before been performed—propitiating the Economy while hacking away at the Deficit that clings to its back. In other words, he has to use government to "grow the economy," while simultaneously shrinking the government. This is more or less like slaying the dragon at the same time that one swallows one's sword.

At last it is "Economy night." The speech itself sounds eerily familiar, if only because we have heard the prespeech plus a thousand leaks and prognostications. To placate the middle class, Clinton promises to tax the rich. To soothe the rich, he has Hillary sitting between a CEO and the head of the Federal Reserve Board, symbolizing the continuing reign of the money men. Furthermore, he asserts that the role of government is to serve the Economy in a modest and unobtrusive fashion—supplying navigable roads, for example, and workers who can count to high numbers. This is not quite the withering-away-of-the-state as promised by Ronald Reagan, but it's close: 100,000 federal workers will be laid off to reduce the deficit, which at the same time will be mightily increased by tax cuts for business designed to—weirdly enough—generate employment.

Afterward, cagey pundits are unwilling to commit themselves. How can they know what to make of the plan until the polls have been taken and processed? In the White House they are already drafting the Presidential Address on the Economy III.

[1992]

Gone with the Wind

Not so long ago the weather was just an innocent conversational filler. "Cold enough for you?" the neighbor would inquire with an evil grin. "Well, yes," you'd allow—minus 10 degrees plus 70 mph gusts will pretty much do the trick. Now however the weather has gotten so perverse that one hesitates to bring the subject up, for fear that the children might be listening.

Well, how do you explain a forecast of hurricanes combined with snow and tornadoes and possible torrents of frogs? New words were required—"snowicane," "blizzicane"—though none of them quite captures the apocalyptic frisson of watching the snow drift silently over one's buried car while thunder clatters overhead.

We were a little skeptical, I will admit, when we sat down to watch it on TV. The older, more sophisticated children grumped about all the attention being paid to the weather— "I mean, in this day and age." You do tend to forget about the weather, as if it were some oafish, half-retarded second cousin who has long since been overshadowed by his far brighter siblings—War and Plague. Why watch the weather, the kids were saying, when we could be watching AIDS or ethnic cleansing?

But the media threw themselves open-armed into the oncoming wind. Storm of the century! they told us. Bigger than Bosnia! No matter what channel we watched, a little band of print would appear at the bottom of the screen, warning of disaster and—what is often worse—hours of detailed coverage to come. There wasn't much else in the news, after all, except for Yeltsin's ingenious plan to advance democracy by imposing one-man rule, but the visuals for that were just too dreary: whole acres of overweight, middle-aged white men in suits.

On Friday night, with Storm of the Century only a few states away, we ventured out for basic supplies. Unfortunately, everyone else had the same idea, and bedlam reigned in the video store. Good people, nonviolent, lawn-maintaining types, were battling each other over the few remaining tapes—exercise videos, National Geographic specials, and several offerings involving Bruce Willis. Forget about it, the husband advised, we'll just stick to the Weather Channel.

Yes, our home now has the Weather Channel, offering 24-hour-a-day reports on the temperature in Lone Pine and the barometric pressure in downtown Akron, and interrupted by commercials exactly like normal programming. In fact, well before Storm of the Century, the weather—like so many things in our postmodern age—had been moving steadily out of the realm of necessity and into the far cheerier realm of the spectacle. Increasingly, one finds the weatherman sitting side by side with the anchorpersons, engaging in timely bits of banter. No one found it odd that the movie *Groundhog Day* featured a celebrity weatherman made insufferably arrogant by excessive acclaim.

Soon we can expect the pundits to start moving in on the weather and putting an ideological spin on meteorological issues. Admirers of untrammeled free enterprise will no doubt welcome every storm with gusto, exposing their pallid chests to the breeze. On the far left, or its TV equivalent, there will be timorous murmurings about how, if the public sector hadn't been entirely gutted in the last twelve years of Republican rule, there might still be money for snowplows, etc. Think-tank residents who have bored us for years with their snappy prognostications will instead debate three inches or two, followed by sun or hail.

Storm of the Century didn't let us down. All weekend, over pizza and popcorn, we watched beach homes float out to sea, multimillion-dollar yachts gurgle and sink, snowdrifts envelop little-known towns. It's not all fun, we grimly reminded the kids. Think of the lives lost, the ruined crops, the roofless homes. Not to mention the hundreds of thousands who lost their electricity and hence, tragically, spent the weekend in darkness, missing the entire thing.

[1993]

Readers' Block

Every now and then some new scientific finding comes along that explains, potentially, everything. Why, for example, restaurant menus are increasingly rendered in pictograms, so the customer need only point with a finger and grunt. Why a book can be a "best-seller" with sales in the high four-figure range, and why so many of our elected officials resemble in-patients on a scheduled outing. I could go on and on with the disparate facts that have finally fallen into place, now that a U.S. Education Department study has found that 50 percent of Americans are illiterate. And since the same percent cannot do elementary arithmetic, and since some of them are no doubt employed by the Education Department itself, the real number may be far higher—57 percent or possibly 90.

Naturally, my colleagues in the print industry want someone to blame, and they are lashing out at the usual suspects: underfunded schools, TV, improperly fitted contact lenses, accumulated lead in the brain.

But the truth is far simpler. The truth is that 50 percent of Americans have tried reading, and have given it up. Oh, they *can* read, or at least could years ago when they finished fourth grade. But they soon found that there's nothing worth reading, at least nothing within easy reach.

Consider that daily intrusion of waste paper still wistfully known as the "mail." Once that word signified scented billets-doux and long soulful epistles from friends. Today it is likely to mean an assortment of apocalyptic warnings ("In the time it takes you to toss out this envelope, 500 more acres of rain forest will be transformed into parking lots . . .") and thinly veiled threats ("Perhaps you misplaced last month's invoice . . ."). Somewhere within this pile lies the largest assemblage of print the average person is ever likely to find in one place—the tiny gray letters on the back of a credit-card bill, advising:

Each day, take the sum of all Advances or debit adjustments which appeared on the previous statement and are now part of the Previous Balance, "One Cycle Advances . . ." Add all of the daily amounts together. This is the sum of all "One Cycle Advances." Add the sum of each category together and . . .

Or consider that bible of the "computer-literate" stratum, *The DOS Manual.* What is DOS? Does anybody actually know? Opening my own manual at random, I find, "The syntax for the PRINT command is PRINT /B:bufsize /D:device /M:maxtick /S:timeslice/ U:busytick d:paths filename.ext /T/C/P . . ."

But, of course, why PRINT? Everywhere one looks, proofs of the futility of literacy fly into one's face. Pick up a newspaper, and there is always the danger of encountering a summary of the Clinton health plan, which—with its multiple layers of overlapping and intersecting bureaucracies—cannot even be rendered in linear text, but requires a multidimensional hyperspace computerized projection.

I myself have almost given up on reading. It was a communication from the IRS that did me in, or possibly some incredible claim about unpaid parking tickets. Nowadays, confronted with any bureaucratic form, I zoom right down to the spot where my X is required. It may be that as a result I have confessed to dozens of crimes I did not commit, but frying in the electric chair is small price to pay for the freedom from reading fine print.

Most people have figured out by now that print is the medium of intimidation, expropriation, and threat. When someone has something nice to say, they say it with pictures or flowers or strippers-by-wire. But when there's nastiness afoot, which is most of the time, the forewarning always comes in cold print. Thus TV, which is our friend, does not assault us with words, while the Welfare Department, which wishes us dead, does not communicate with jolly cartoons.

The problem, then, is not that people are dumb. The problem is that, in late-corporate-capitalist-bureaucratic society, there is not a whole lot one would willingly read. And most of the things that one really should read, such as the "mail," are so relentlessly hostile to the human spirit that refusing to read may be the only dignified course of action. So mass illiteracy must be seen for what it is—a quiet, but determined, postmodern rebellion.

[1993]

Camelot Redux

A friend calls to tell me she has dreamed that Bill Clinton was assassinated. Don't worry, I tell her, Dan Quayle is no longer the veep. That's the problem, she says: Quayle was George Bush's assassination insurance, but what hardworking, principled assassin would be stopped by Al Gore? Besides, she says, lowering her voice, it's the whole Kennedy theme—a frisky young fellow in the White House, a beautiful, intelligent first lady. Camelot, in other words, all over again. Can an assassination be far behind?

So, according to the prevailing metaphors, here we are in 1961 again. The rule of the grandfathers has been overthrown. Hope is in the air. Time, then, for the myth of the doomed young prince who must be sacrificed for all our sins. And it makes a certain amount of sense: did not the teenage Clinton shake the hand of JFK himself, thus allowing for the transmission of the tragic script? In fact, there was no real reason to have an inauguration when we could have proceeded at once to the grassy knoll or the Texas School Book Depository.

Déjà vu, once a difficult, esoteric concept known only to Proust scholars and speakers of French, is now such a numbing cliché that to hear it is to experience it—as in "déjà vu all over again." Everything that happens, we are led to believe, is a historical reenactment on a par with Williamsburg, Virginia. Clinton is Kennedy, Bush was Nixon, Reagan was a hologram out of the Hollywood past. Let people with picket signs appear on TV, and the voice-over inevitably brings up the 1960s. Everything is a rerun and not just on summer TV.

No doubt it is comforting to think that the future holds no surprises, only programs we have seen before. A certain smugness sets in as the pundits announce our arrival on schedule right where we used to be. If the 1990s are supposed to mimic the 1960s, this is because most Americans subscribe to a thirty-year-cycle theory of history: First there is an action-packed decade—the 1930s for example, with marches and strikes, or the 1960s, with mass movements and reduced standards of personal hygiene. Then we get a couple of sluggish, reactionary, event-free decades in which everyone catches their breath before starting all over again. So if this is 1993, can 1964 be far behind?

It's not just that "history repeats." In the conventional, media view, it barely happens at all anymore. Once, long ago, there was history, and way before that there was prehistory. But now there is only re-history.

Europe would seem to be a perfect example. Once a bustling, forward-looking place, its citizens have gone back to wearing lederhosen and searching for any leftover Jews to torment. Sarajevo, concentration camps: who would have thought they'd be back so fast? Germany in particular seems to be running on instant replay: Nazis firebombing "undesirables." Anarchists, filling in for the Communists of pre-Hitler days, battling Nazis in the streets—all while a feeble, vacillating government looks on. Or consider the post-Communist world, which is busy reinventing capitalism—along with mass unemployment, hunger, and Stalin-nostalgia cults. If you miss Communism, just wait a minute. It'll be back in a week or two.

Now, of course, the second law of thermodynamics forbids the literal repetition of history, even as farce. Clinton is not Kennedy: he's fitter, for one thing, and nowhere near as funny. Kohl's Germany is not the Weimar Republic but a historical novelty: a fat bourgeois nation (the former West) onto which a vast lower class (the former East) was appended almost overnight, with predictably hideous social tensions as a result. Nor is the post-Communist world—from Serbia to Azerbaijan—a cryonically preserved fossil which is just now thawing out and preparing to enter the 1930s again. The peoples of the Communist world have been doing *something* for the past fifty years—thinking something, evolving in their own peculiar direction—and the sooner we understand what that was all about, the better off we are all likely to be.

The fact that nothing seems to be happening, that things seem only to be re-happening, may be an artifact of the VCR. Once it was possible to "miss" a movie: it came to the theater, and then it was gone. Now, however, all things—or at least all images, scenes, gestures, and other tidbits of cultural bricolage—are with us at all times, or only a flick of a switch away. How many times I have ventured near the TV, only to have a family member call out gaily, "Hey Mom, it's the face-eating scene from Cape Fear—wanna see it again?" Because if you liked it the first time, you'll like it again, and again. At live family gatherings, we videotape our initial awkward and testy interactions, pop the tape in the VCR, and sit back to relive the last twenty minutes.

The idea that real events operate much the same way is not only boring but dangerous. If history is an amusement-park ride rushing us through preordained thrills—fascism! the 1960s! and so forth—then there's nothing we can do but hold tight and squeal. Fatalism takes over—a chic fin de siècle withdrawal from actual engagement in the world as it actually is, which is endlessly strange and surprising.

The notion of history has to be particularly oppressive to the young. Ever since the demise of the yuppie, eager journalists have been announcing a "new generation" with "new values" and intriguing new notions of what constitutes fun. First it was to be the "cautious" postfeminist generation, then a cohort of young environmentalists in grunge garb, or maybe ravers cavorting on Ecstasy. But one by one, these waves of twenty-somethings have peeked out for a moment and then crept quietly off into middle age. Why don't they do anything bold or interesting? Because they have been raised to believe that all those things have been done before, and probably by their very own parents. If you want miniskirts and Vietnam, they figure, you can always rent the tape.

I understand that our media people have only a limited supply of myths and images to feed us. I understand, too, the need to be an expert on whatever is happening, chiefly by virtue of having seen it all before. But the public and especially its younger members should demand a future of their own— one that does not require the assassination of Bill Clinton, the rebirth of Nazism, or rebels wearing feathers and beads.

[1993]

Star Power

One billion people watched the Academy Awards in 1993, the highest number ever. Serbian irregulars tuned in on borrowed Muslim TV sets. Shantytown dwellers in Santiago gathered to see Billy Crystal in a tux that resembled a Catwoman suit. Bedouins marveled at the colony of pink sea anemones growing from Catherine Deneuve's chest. Not that the show was entertaining; it had all the flaws of your standard Hollywood production—too long by at least three hours, scripted by a staff of lower primates, and, of course, highly derivative of other movies. No, we watch for what might be called political reasons: because everyone knows that the movie-star class now rules the earth.

Consider the telling moment when Richard Gere, famed Buddhist and part-time priapist, took the podium to scold Deng Xiaoping, a mere head-of-state. Or there was the ancient lounge lizard Jack Valenti, boasting that—despite hideously unfair competition from *Howards End* and *The Crying Game*—Hollywood had saved the U.S. balance of payments.

Once it was the capitalists who occupied center stage in the world's affairs, but they were—what shall we say?—not exactly a camera-ready bunch, with their uniformly bloated white male faces. No one was interested in their sex lives, their fitness regimes, or whether they had been molested as tots. Worse yet, they were poor. Or so we discovered when, after the first mild protests over seven-figure executive salaries, the CEOs all stamped their feet and pointed to the eight-figure paychecks routinely raked in by the likes of Madonna and Arnold Schwarzenegger.

Steadily over the years, the movie-star class has been consolidating its power. While other American industries began to slough off their employees like so many head lice, movie stars picked up the slack, providing employment to whole armies of assistants, subassistants, eyebrow pluckers, plastic surgeons, personal trainers, bodyguards, food tasters, leg shavers. And, like the European royal families long before them, they intermarried and inbred, guaranteeing that their power would remain forever within the caste. We have Anjelica, daughter of John; Michael, son of Kirk; Bridget, daughter of Peter; Charlie, son of Martin; etc., etc.—to the point where one cannot see a happy Hollywood couple like Tim Robbins and Susan Sarandon without wondering whether the children will have her face or (God help us) his, and whether we will ever have to see them bare-breasted.

So the grand progress of Western civilization should now be apparent: First there was the feudal aristocracy, whose power rested in control of the Land. Next came the capitalist class, which controlled the Means of Production. And now, in line with the general postmodern drift from production to simulation, from the tangible to the virtual, we have the movie-star class, with its absolute ownership of Image and Gesture.

Never was the power of the movie-star class more recklessly displayed than in the last presidential election. George Bush, still living in a bygone era, surrounded himself with CEOs, Wall Street felons, real estate speculators, and other remnants of the declining capitalist class. Bill Clinton, far craftier, donned his Ray-Bans and played the sax. The true inauguration, as everyone knows, was not the ghastly noontime ritual presided over by men in medieval robes. No, the real one had occurred the night before, when Bill Cosby lectured Bill and Al on remaining in touch with the common man and Barbra Streisand sang to them sweetly about the importance of being nice to children.

But the awards ceremony itself was a harsh lesson in movie-star power. While Crystal engaged in his usual low-IQ banter with Jack Palance, whole communities of Zulus and Shintoists tore out their hair. Germans swilled beer, and Egyptians smoked hash, to get through the many life-sapping episodes of song and dance. It is even rumored that a whole village of starving Somalians gave up the ghost rather than hear one more sound director or makeup artist thank his or her ancestors, neighbors, and cousins. What could be a more brutal display of naked power than to gather up one-fourth of the planet's inhabitants and bore them to the edge of despair?

[1993]

Won't Somebody

Do Something Silly?

For a moment we seemed to be on the verge of a major new trend, the theme of which was angels. People were snapping up angel pins and wearing them on their shoulders, where normally the chip is carried. Soon, the trend spotters hoped, there would be a rage for choir music, angel food cake, and Marshmallow Fluff. Huge feathery wings would sprout out from trench coats and parkas. But, alas, angels sputtered and stalled and never quite got off the ground.

Possibly related is the failure of the great altruism trend to appear on schedule. As predicted by Arthur Schlesinger, Jr., and others, the 1980s were supposed to be followed by something closely resembling the 1960s: concern for the underdog, public nudity, giving all for the cause. Perhaps it just seemed too overwhelming—considering that to balance the greed of the eighties commuters would have had to strip the very coats from their backs and donate them to unwashed vagrants, along with the keys to their country homes. So the altruism trend, along with the angels, remains a gleam in the trend watcher's eye.

Once America was the great exporter of trends—not just fads, like multiple earrings and cholesterol anxiety, but whole new life-styles involving characteristic garments, attitudes, and substances of choice. In 1967, for example, the first hippies were detected in San Francisco, and within a year the historic fountains of Europe were crowded with pot-smoking young people clad only in tattoos. In 1984 America produced the first yuppies, who have since moved on to infest London and Frankfurt. Why, the very concept of "life-style" is an American invention, implying that there is more than one choice.

But there hasn't been a serious life-style trend since the couch potato was sighted, in about 1986, on one of its rare forays to the video store. Cocooning remains a significant mass enterprise, encouraged by the availability of five hundred new cable channels and microwavable popcorn. But if you want an outdoor trend, one that demands emulation and is inspired by zest rather than a fear of human interaction and bizarre weather events, then there is nothing at all. The only trend worth mentioning is trendlessness.

This is hard on journalists, who are trained to spot trendlets in their infancy and hype them into vast cultural sea changes. Not too long ago for instance, *Time* magazine announced a "new simplicity" trend involving antimaterialism and wood-burning stoves—but the new simplicity turned out to be only the old recession. Or there was CBS's pitiful attempt to claim alternative healing as a newsworthy trend. Healing with crystals and chamomile may have been trendy and exciting in 1974. Today, among the 37 million uninsured, chamomile has long since replaced penicillin, and going to an internist is considered a form of "alternative healing."

All right, there have been a few certifiable trendlets here and there—inflatable bikinis, Virgin Mary sightings, potato-spelling jokes—but most were too sickly and feeble to grow. Divorcing one's parents looked big for a week or so, sparking hopes of a real estate boom as ten-year-olds sought their own condos. Menopause mania proved to be a flash, so to speak, in the pan, and "smart drugs" couldn't compete with the far more numerous dumb ones.

Obviously there are still deep underlying trends, indicative of seismic-scale cultural drift. Assisted suicide, for example. Abandoning the elderly in their wheelchairs. Intergenerational downward mobility. But these are not the kind of things one would want to see spread around the world like hula hoops, stamped MADE IN THE USA. The same goes for the cannibalism trend as promoted by Anthony Hopkins. Not to mention *Studs*-like game shows, in which attractive young people make witty remarks about body parts.

There hasn't even been a political trend worth mentioning—the last presidential election signaling less a leftward trend than a rejection of the rightward trend that has been slithering around for two decades now. As a result we've been forced to import trends, like karaoke, or revive fossil trends like troll dolls, which first showed their wizened little rubber faces almost thirty years ago. In the realm of dessert, the only happening thing is *tiramisú*, which comes to us from Italy via a brief craze in Japan. Even our gossip often has to be imported now, since we lack a homegrown equivalent of the topless, toe-sucking, dysfunctional royals.

Perhaps we should welcome the posttrend era. We no longer rush off, herdlike, to become Jesus freaks or Val gals at the first hint from the national media. It takes maturity to see a fetching new image—say Madonna in gold tooth and riding crop—without thinking, "Hey, wow, that could be me!"

But there's something sad, too, about the decline of the American trend industry. Trendsetting requires innovation, ebullience, and a level of defiant frivolity such as has not been seen in these parts for years. Maybe we've had too many presidents with brown-tinted hair and programs distilled from focus groups. Maybe, two years into a recession, we're just too anxious and overworked for naked roller-blading and whole-body tattoos. Or perhaps cocooning was by its nature the ultimate and final trend, after which no more trends are biologically possible: like the dodo snuggling into its nest, we have found our evolutionary niche, which turns out to be the couch in the den.

Patriotism demands at least one more world-shaking, American-made trend. Surely the nation that invented goldfish swallowing and the leisure suit is not willing to exit the millennium watching reruns on Nick At Night. Arise, ye pallid twenty-somethings, and do something deeply silly!

[1993]

The Blight of
the Living Dead

Things have been moving a little too fast on the techno-front. First there was *Jurassic Park*, where the big breakthrough was not the synthesis of dinosaurs from bits of amber and frog eggs (scientists do that kind of thing every day now). No, the really scary thing is that the dinosaurs so generated were not even fake, like Godzilla; they were actually, so to speak, virtual. All those brachiosauruses and velociraptors were in fact computer simulations superimposed on some tiresome footage of a bunch of people tearing around the jungle and screeching at nothing more terrifying than a camera crew.

Then we read about the new "information highway" coming our way. According to the advance reports, you will be connected to the highway via a "teleputer" containing your TV, fax machine, personal computer, telephone, and probably toaster, and tiny enough to be lodged in a dental filling. Already in Seattle, we are told, "people can get weather forecasts, market quotes, ski reports, sports scores, all transmitted . . . to displays on their Seiko watches." If they need to know the time, of course, they are advised to search out a sundial.

But think of it! There you will be, thanks to your watch or dental filling as the case may be, standing in the path of this huge gushing river of information containing everything that has ever been on television, or in a movie or book, or on a disk or database of any kind. Bits of info pelting you from all directions: the price of a lovely ankle bracelet from the Home Shopping Channel, the margin on pork bellies from the Chicago Stock Market, reruns of *Gilligan's Island*, the cube root of 17, major league batting averages going back to 1937.

And you will be a part of it, this mighty flow! For one thing, it will all be interactive, we are promised, so you are free to edit and modify the info as it rushes along: Want to see *Jurassic Park* with turkeys playing the part of the dinosaurs? Go right ahead. Prefer that the cube root of 17 be a nice easy-to-remember integer like 3? Be my guest.

Plus remember that computers will have merged with TV sets, so that your checkbook-balancing program and the sonnet you were writing in your spare time will all be joyously commingling with everything from *Beverly Hills 90210* to the weather report for Reykjavík. All the information that has ever existed will be yours, in whatever form you want it—true, false, colorized, or otherwise improved!

There will be problems, of course. It may be necessary to lug around a 500-pound electron microscope in order to view the tiny screen of your teleputer. Not to mention that it will be slow work loading the fax paper into an object that can be manipulated only with tweezers. And in order to use the teleputer's teensy keyboard, we may need to grow long whisker-like filaments out of our fingertips.

But these are minor, engineering-type problems. Far more worrisome is the question of what happens when you have zillions of info-bytes rushing around in something the size of a tooth filling. Recall the philosophical message of *Jurassic Park*: Anything that can happen will—this is the word from "chaos theory." T. Rex will chew its way loose. Females will metamorphose into males. Dino embryos will spill on the jungle floor, providing the basis for *Jurassic Park II.*

So think of what could happen when chaos theory gets its hands on the information highway. Reruns of *The Night of the Living Dead* bleeding into C-Span presentations of Congress in session. Velociraptors getting out of *Jurassic Park* and mating with that memo you were planning to send to the boss. The checkbook-balancing program merging with the evil lawyers from *The Firm* and embezzling your life savings . . .

But there's no reason to worry, is there, if the whole thing is sufficiently interactive? Just pump your bank balance up to the desired number and let the velociraptor-memo-hybrid eat the boss. There'll be no need for further unpleasantness when we're all drifting peacefully down the great interactive information highway to hallucinatory bliss.

[1993]

Paying Attention to O.J.

Someday my grandchildren will gather around and ask where I was and what I was doing when I learned of O. J. Simpson's escape from the police. I will gnaw reflectively on the handle of my cane and tell them that I was watching the big basketball game, like any good citizen, since I had taken that to be the event du jour. See, in those days, I will have to explain, we periodically had some event du jour—a war, a penisectomy, a figure skater run amok—just to see if everyone was paying attention. And woe to the distracted or derelict citizen who could not pass the follow-up quiz, administered by selected neighbors: "Hey, whaddya think of them Knicks?" or "So O.J.—think he did it, huh?"

So I had been watching the game, trying to guess what would be on the next morning's quiz, when suddenly the screen was taken over by O.J.'s getaway car gliding along empty freeways, pursued by a flock of press helicopters. Suspecting that some typical postnuclear-holocaust action film had drifted in from another channel, I frantically clicked the remote. But O.J. was everywhere and inescapable, supposedly sitting in the backseat with a gun to his head, though possibly it was a cellular phone or even a cordless shaver.

At first I was so clueless I confused O.J. with Jackie O.— and, in fact, there is a certain resemblance. Struggling to explain the historic importance of O.J., the newspeople kept coming up with the same content-free terms they had applied to Jackie O.—"grace," "role model," and "bone structure." In short, O.J., like the nebulous J.O., is famous principally for being a celebrity. He played football at one point, but is best known for the Hertz commercial in which he vaults over airport counters and mounds of fellow passengers in his eagerness to rent a car.

Thus the chase theme was wonderfully appropriate, as the anchorpersons' voice-overs kept reminding us. And was this not the primal experience of advanced capitalism—senseless, undirected flight? The excitement mounted as O.J.'s car approached the Los Angeles airport: maybe he would leap out and offer a live replay of the famed Hertz commercial, only this time going from car to plane. Never before had we seen all the possible genres—news, sports, docudramas, and commercials—merge in such a brilliant conflation.

It was overwhelming to be "participating," as Peter Jennings put it, in the making of a major media event. A local L.A. reporter broke down, choking and hanging his head, while an anchorman's voice murmured apologetically about "the stress we've been through." Thousands of Angelenos were shown massing along the freeways, thrilled, as some said, to be "part of history." They sobbed, embraced one another, chanted encouragement to O.J., swilled beer, and thought of good places to loot. Everywhere, Americans felt themselves caught up in the kind of vast maudlin seizure that leads us periodically to folly and war.

In those days, I'll explain to the grandkids, we were starved for any sort of tribal experience. We lived each shut up in our single-family homes, yearning for an outbreak of communal drumming and dancing or perhaps a spectacular blood sacrifice. Hence the necessity of these events du jour to periodically uplift us from the trivial and the personal into the plane of the historic and transcendent. In this, O.J. was wildly successful, achieving ratings that rivaled the Gulf War. He even won the newsperson's ultimate accolade: he "brought us together."

And that's what it was all about—synchronization. Everyone watching the same thing at the same time, saying the same dumb things, guzzling the same brand of beer. We really didn't care what inspired them, so deeply did we crave these collective highs. Give us a war, we would cry—a shuttle blowing up, an assassination, a runaway rental car spokesman!

At which the grandchildren will no doubt shake their heads in wonder, throw a few more twigs on the campfire, and hunker down on the ground for the night.

[1994]

The Triumph of Trash

The annual season of media breast-beating is in full swing. Gennifer Flowers inspired the last one; Paula Jones and O.J. set off this year's round of confessions and recriminations. In the wake of the Jones minifuss, media heavies such as Dan Rather have been sniffing noisily about all the silly, ephemeral stuff that has come to constitute news. Even the sober *New York Times* convened a roundtable of journalists to moan about the encroachment of sleaze. Random readers and viewers also claim to be horrified at the lurid turn the news has taken, as if to say, "Gee, I'd rather be reading about GATT."

But who are we kidding? Trash news triumphs because trash is fun. Give me a choice between a half-page analysis of The Law of the Sea and a fresh outbreak of serial cannibalism, and I know where my eye will settle. If it's Hillary's 1,300-page health proposal versus Lorena's amateur surgery, health reform will have to wait. Maybe the taste for trash is hard-wired into the human brain. Sex and violence are mind-candy, while "hard" news—from interest rates to human rights in China —is the mental equivalent of fiber.

Nor is there any mystery why the media cater to the human appetite for trash. Almost all our news comes from commercial, profit-seeking enterprises. The journalist's goal may be to educate and inform, but the company's goal is to sell a "media product." If O.J. moves the product, then he will lead the news, while the Mexican election sediments into a footnote-sized item on page 32. This has nothing to do with the individual depravity of media folk, though that can never be entirely ruled out. It's just the iron law of the market. Even the breast-beating has become a predictable part of the media spectacle, according to University of California media critic Todd Gitlin—a "ritual of public expiation."

Sex scandals are only the tip of the media trash heap. More and more of the "news" is of the juicy, premasticated, viewer-friendly variety. When we're not reading about Erik and Lyle, we're gobbling up grotesque local crime stories, sycophantic celebrity interviews, or trashlike "news" about the media themselves. Consider the tumorous growth of "entertainment news." Once restricted to *Entertainment Tonight* and a few other limited venues, it's been steadily taking over the six o'clock news, where we're now far more likely to find out what miniseries is playing at nine than what happened to the local bond issue.

Or we get "hard" news tarted up as low-grade trash: Clinton's nomination of Stephen Breyer presented, on ABC's evening news, as a drama of male bonding and athleticism, Hillary's political fortunes as seen through her evolving hair. If the subject is welfare, the focus will be on "illegitimacy," drugs, and babies abandoned in roach-infested apartments—all of which are a lot more mind-grabbing than concepts like class polarization and structural unemployment.

The obvious trend, which has been noted before, is toward the merger of news and entertainment. We have news about entertainment, and we have news *as* entertainment. No one is forced to read *The Economist* as opposed to *US*, or choose *MacNeil-Lehrer* over *Geraldo*. So the formerly distinguishable categories of news and entertainment begin to blend into one continuous, and continually seductive, media blur.

But the underlying, and ultimately far more sinister, trend is for the news media to give the public exactly what it wants. And since the networks and major newspapers developed their own polling services in the mid-1970s, it has become far easier to know what that is. Media polling is done in part because poll data are considered "news." But polling also serves to guide media executives in making assignments and ranking stories. Some of the TV-magazine and public-affairs shows have even taken to monitoring viewer reactions minute by minute—as the show is being aired—and can, in principle, switch from Bosnia to the Bobbitts the moment the remotes start clicking.

The not-so-distant sci-fi result will be *interactive* news. We like to think there's a flow of information that goes from the "real world," then out through the filtering and sorting mechanisms of the media, and on into the expectant mind of the public. What we're approaching instead is a closed loop, with the "news" flowing in one direction while the ratings and poll data flow the other way, back to the news writers and news makers. In a closed circuit, bizarre feedback phenomena easily take over. During the eighties for example, opinion makers determined that "drugs"—or, at one point, "terrorism"—was our leading problem, and the media eagerly hyped the issue du jour. Not surprisingly, the polls soon showed the public concurring. So the media offered more crack babies to keep up with the demand (though drug use in general was declining); the polls showed ever-mounting interest and alarm; and so on . . . into the dark night of mass, onanistic delusion.

What journalists ought to be worried about is how they are going to make a living in the interactive, fun-news future. The journalist's traditional function was to select and spin the stories that come to be known as the news. But when the news is selected on the basis of crude, instantaneous reactions, then computers might as well do the job. Mr. Joe Q. Public will just sit down at his CD-ROM, call up some titillating celebrity gossip, scare himself with a few slasher stories, or perhaps decide to watch Rwanda—only with a happy ending of his own design.

[1994]

THE

SNARLING

CITIZEN

Teach Diversity—

with a Smile

Something had to replace the threat of Communism, and at last a workable substitute is at hand. "Multiculturalism," as the new menace is known, has been denounced in the media as the new McCarthyism, the new fundamentalism, even the new totalitarianism—take your choice. According to its critics, who include a flock of tenured conservative scholars, multiculturalism aims to toss out what it sees as the Eurocentric bias in education and to replace Plato with Ntozake Shange and traditional math with the Yoruba number system. And that's just the beginning. The Jacobins of the multiculturalist movement, who are described derisively as p.c., or politically correct, are said to have launched a campus reign of terror against those who slip and innocently say "freshman" instead of "freshperson," "Indian" instead of "Native American," or, may the Goddess forgive them, "disabled" instead of "differently abled."

So you can see what is at stake here: freedom of speech, freedom of thought, Western civilization, and a great many professorial egos. But before we get carried away by the mounting backlash against multiculturalism, we ought to reflect for a moment on the system that the p.c. people aim to replace.

I know all about it; in fact, it's just about all I *do* know, since I—along with so many educated white people of my generation—was a victim of monoculturalism.

American history, as it was taught to us, began with Columbus's "discovery" of an apparently unnamed, unpeopled America, and moved on to the Pilgrims serving pumpkin pie to a handful of grateful red-skinned folks. College expanded our horizons with courses called Humanities or sometimes Civ, which introduced us to a line of thought that started with Homer, worked its way through Rabelais, and reached a poignant climax in the pensées of Matthew Arnold. Graduate students wrote dissertations on what long-dead men had thought of Chaucer's verse or Shakespeare's dramas; foreign languages meant French or German. If there had been high technology in ancient China, kingdoms in black Africa, or women anywhere, at any time, doing anything worth noticing, we did not know it, nor did anyone think to tell us.

Our families and neighborhoods reinforced the dogma of monoculturalism. In our heads, most of us 1950s teenagers carried around a social map that was about as useful as the chart that guided Columbus to the "Indies." There were "Negroes," "whites," and "Orientals," the latter meaning Chinese and "Japs." Of religions, only three were known—Protestant, Catholic, and Jewish—and not much was known about the last two types. The only remaining human categories were husbands and wives, and that was all the diversity the monocultural world could handle. Gays, lesbians, Buddhists, Muslims, Malaysians, Mormons, etc. were simply off the map.

So I applaud—with one hand, anyway—the multiculturalist goal of preparing us all for a wider world. The other hand is tapping its fingers impatiently, because the critics are right about one thing: when advocates of multiculturalism adopt the haughty stance of political correctness, they quickly descend to silliness or worse. It's obnoxious, for example, to rely on university administrations to enforce p.c. standards of verbal inoffensiveness. Racist, sexist, and homophobic thoughts, alas, can be abolished not by fiat but only by the time-honored methods of persuasion, education, and exposure to the other guy's—or, excuse me, woman's—point of view.

And it's silly to mistake verbal purification for genuine social reform. Even after all women are "Ms." and all people are "he or she," women will still earn only sixty-five cents for every dollar earned by men. Minorities by any other name, such as "people of color," will still bear a hugely disproportionate burden of poverty and discrimination. Disabilities are not just "different abilities" when there are not enough ramps for wheelchairs, signers for the deaf, or special classes for the "specially" endowed. With all due respect for the new politesse, actions still speak louder than fashionable phrases.

But the worst thing about the p.c. people is that they are such poor advocates for the multicultural cause. No one was ever won over to a broader, more inclusive view of life by being bullied or relentlessly "corrected." Tell a nineteen-year-old white male that he can't say "girl" when he means "teenage woman," and he will most likely snicker. This may be the reason why, despite the conservative alarms, p.c.-ness remains a relatively tiny trend. Most campuses have more serious and ancient problems: faculties still top-heavy with white males of the monocultural persuasion; fraternities that harass minorities and women; date rape; alcohol abuse; and tuition that excludes all but the upper fringe of the middle class.

So both sides would be well advised to lighten up. The conservatives ought to realize that criticisms of the great books approach to learning do not amount to totalitarianism. And the advocates of multiculturalism need to regain the sense of humor that enabled their predecessors in the struggle to coin the term p.c. years ago—not in arrogance but in self-mockery.

Beyond that, both sides should realize that the beneficiaries of multiculturalism are not only the "oppressed peoples" on the standard p.c. list (minorities, gays, etc.). The "unenlightened"—the victims of monoculturalism—are oppressed too, or at least deprived. Our educations, whether at Yale or at State U, were narrow and parochial and left us ill-equipped to navigate a society that truly is multicultural and is becoming more so every day. The culture that we studied was, in fact, *one* culture and, from a world perspective, all too limited and ingrown. Diversity is challenging, but those of us who have seen the alternative know it is also richer, livelier, and, ultimately, more fun.

[1991]

Down to

the Fundamentals

I am often approached on the street by gaggles of Euro-tourists wanting to know what it's like, living in a Christian nation—or, er, Judeo-Christian, they tactfully add. Their curiosity is understandable, coming as they do from cultures where churchgoing has long since been relegated to the elderly and infirm, and where the Virgin Mary is not given to manifesting herself in the smoke from suburban barbecues. Possibly these tourists have even read a little Scripture and formed a picture in their minds of hordes of eager penitents rushing about the streets, desperate to dispose of their worldly goods. Naturally they are hesitant to venture out alone, for fear of being accosted by Christians anxious to unload their wallets and shed the very shirts on their backs.

Is it a problem getting from one place to another, the Eurotourists want to know—what with all the Christians crowding around, offering to drive you or pay your fare? No problem at all, I tell them, trying not to smirk at the ignorance of our foreign guests. Christianity has progressed, I explain; it has evolved along with everything else. Once Christians worried about getting through the eye of a needle with their fur coats on and stacks of Vuitton luggage in tow. Now they worry about serious things like being boiled alive by witches.

Boiled? A pallor comes over the handsome tan faces of my Eurofriends. Well, of course. I reach into my pocket and fish out a slim volume of Christian thought. Here, I say, listen to the words of our great Christian leader and media mogul, Pat Robertson, founder of the Christian Coalition and featured speaker at the Republican National Convention. He says that feminism is "a socialist, anti-family political movement that encourages women to leave their husbands, kill their children, practice witchcraft, destroy capitalism, and become lesbians."

Are there many of these feminists? the Eurotypes want to know. Yep, I tell them darkly: polls show that about 70 percent of American women believe the nation needs "a strong women's movement"—meaning that the overwhelming majority of American women would like to cook up their children and use the resulting broth as a potion to transform the stockbroker class into a swarm of green frogs.

The tourists are now nervously consulting their Air France schedules. But that's nothing, I warn them, compared to the gay threat. Gay . . . *threat?* they ask, clearly confused by this novel conjuncture of concepts. So I flip through my book of Christian thought to the words of that other fine Christian leader, the Reverend Lou Sheldon of the Traditional Values Coalition in Anaheim, California, home of the original Disneyland. Gays, he says, support "sex with animals and the rape of children as forms of political expression." Not to mention their plan to infiltrate the armed forces and replace the standard khaki uniform with something involving sequins and G-strings.

What about the down-and-out, the Europests are now demanding, pointing to the ragged creatures sleeping underfoot. Aren't Christians supposed to dedicate themselves to the poor, the oppressed, and the sore-afflicted? Strategic realignment, I explain. Jesus hung with prostitutes, beggars, and the otherwise sore-afflicted, and look where that got him. As our modern Christian leaders realize, it's always wiser to consort with the afflictors rather than the sore-afflicted, with the up-and-coming rather than the down-and-out. Hence the modern Christian hierarchy: male over female, straight over gay, rich over poor, etc. Victims are popular too—victims of abortion, child pornography, and witchcraft, that is. But if there's anything a modern Christian loves better than a victim, it is, of course, a bully.

There is a moment of silence, and then the Eurosnobs begin to titter behind their expensively manicured little hands. Well, I snap, is it our fault you sent all your religious nuts here two hundred years ago? Boat after boat full of ranters and ravers and flagellants and fundamentalists? One of the Eurofellows presses a few centimes into my palm, and they all smile indulgently as they head off toward the Statue of Liberty, or Our Lady of the Harbor, as we call her now.

[1992]

Why the Religious Right

Is Wrong

That low moaning sound in the background is the Founding Fathers protesting from beyond the grave. They've been doing it ever since they heard the Republicans announce a "religious war" in the name of "traditional values." It grew several decibels louder when George Bush, at a breakfast of religious leaders, scorched the Democrats for failing to mention God in their platform and declaimed that a president needs to believe in the Almighty. What about the constitutional ban on "religious test[s]" for public office? the Founding Fathers would want to know. What about Tom Jefferson's conviction that it is possible for a nonbeliever to be a moral person, "find[ing] incitements to virtue in the comfort and pleasantness you feel in its exercise"? Even Washington must shudder in his sleep to hear the constant emphasis on "Judeo-Christian values." It was he who wrote, "We have abundant reason to rejoice that in this Land . . . every person may here worship God according to the dictates of his own heart."

George Bush should know better than to encourage the theocratic ambitions of the Christian right. He has claimed—to much snide derision—that when he was shot down in World War II and lay floating in the Pacific he meditated on "God and faith and the separation of church and state." But there could be no better themes for a patriot to address in his final moments. The "wall of separation" the Founding Fathers built between church and state is one of the best defenses freedom ever had.

Or have we already forgotten why the Founding Fathers put it up? They had seen enough religious intolerance in the colonies: Quaker women burned at the stake in Puritan Massachusetts; Virginians liable to be jailed for denying the Bible's authority. They had watched while Europe clawed itself bloody in a series of religious wars recalled now only by their duration—thirty years. No wonder John Adams once described the Judeo-Christian tradition as "the bloodiest religion that ever existed," and that the Founding Fathers took such pains to keep the hand that holds the musket separate from the one that carries the cross.

There was another reason for the separation of church and state, which no amount of pious ranting can expunge: not all the Founding Fathers believed in the same God, or in any God at all. Yes, the Declaration of Independence refers to a deity, but only in the most generic terms—"Nature's God," the "Creator," "Providence"—calculated not to offend the doubters and deists (who believed that God had designed the universe, then left it to nature to run). Jefferson was a renowned doubter, urging his nephew to "question with boldness even the existence of a God." John Adams was at least a skeptic, as were of course the revolutionary firebrands Tom Paine and Ethan Allen. Naturally, they designed a republic in which they themselves would have a place.

For this, today's Republicans should be far more grateful than they are. Abe Lincoln, the patriarch of their party, did not, according to his law partner of twenty-two years, believe in a personal God, and refused to join a church, stating, "When you show me a church based on the Golden Rule as its only creed, then I will unite with it." Ulysses S. Grant, another Republican, exhorted his countrymen to "keep the church and state forever separate" and strongly opposed the use of any public money to support parochial schools—as proposed in the 1992 Republican platform.

But there's another reason for the separation of church and state. If the Founding Fathers had one overarching aim, it was to limit the power not of the churches but of the state. They had seen the abuses of kings who claimed to rule with divine approval—from Henry VIII, who arbitrarily declared himself head of the Church of England, to the high-handed George III. They were deeply concerned, as John Adams wrote, that "government shall be considered as having in it nothing more mysterious or divine than other arts or sciences."

The government the Founding Fathers designed could levy taxes and raise an army, but it could not do these or any other things in the name of a Higher Power. We salute our flag, rather than kneeling before it; our taxes are not called tithes. By stripping government of supernatural authority, the Founding Fathers created a zone of freedom around each individual human conscience—or, for that matter, religious sect. They demystified government, and reduced it to something within reach of human comprehension, protest, and change. Surely the Republicans, committed as they are to "limited government," ought to honor the secular spirit that has limited our government from the moment of its birth.

The same fear of governmental tyranny kept the Founding Fathers from prescribing anything like "family values." Homosexuality was not unknown two hundred years ago, nor was abortion. But these were matters, like religion, that the Founders left to individual conscience. If there was one thing they did believe in, to a man, it was the power of the individual, informed by reason, to decide things for him—or her—self.

Over the years there have been repeated efforts to invest the

U.S. government with the cachet of divine authority. "In God We Trust" was first stamped on currency in the 1860s. "Under God" was inserted into the Pledge of Allegiance during the McCarthyist 1950s. George Bush campaigned in 1988 to have the flag treated as a sacred object. And perhaps every revolution is doomed to be betrayed, sooner or later, by its progeny. It only adds insult to injury, though, when the betrayal is dressed up in the guise of "traditional values."

[1992]

Maintaining

the Crime Supply

It's impossible to address the problem of crime without beginning to worry about the law of supply and demand. Not that many people go around breaking that particular law, but you can be sure we'd get them if they did. Thanks to tough new legislation, we will soon have the most massive and splendid Punishment Industry on earth today: shiny new prisons for every state, harsh new sentences for every infringement, lethal injections more readily available than measles vaccine! Already the United States has a larger proportion of its population locked up than any other nation, South Africa included, so the only worry is—what if we run out of crime?

If punishment actually worked, a crime shortage would develop in no time at all. Would-be criminals would study the available sentences, do a careful cost-benefit analysis, and conclude that armed robbery or, say, aggravated assault just wasn't their cup of tea. Yes, if deterrence worked, as our leaders seem to think it does, we would soon have a vast oversupply of electric chairs and unattractive, heavily walled, rural real estate.

And if crime frightens you, try to imagine a world without a crime. It would be unthinkable: Nothing on TV except

Sesame Street and *Jeopardy* reruns. Chuck Norris reduced to panhandling. No execution tailgate parties, no Court Channel or *NYPD Blue*. Because—let us be honest about it—crime is our favorite entertainment spectacle, crime and punishment, that is. Think how many happy hours the average family spends watching the bad guys get perforated by bullets or menaced by Nazi-biker fiends in the pen.

This is nothing to be ashamed of. Historically, people have long demanded the pleasure of seeing others punished, and usually in live, nonfiction form. Executions were public as a matter of course, providing a festive occasion for the masses. Participatory punishment, in the form of lynchings and stonings, offered the average citizen a vivid, hands-on experience. In fact, historically speaking, the problem has been not to "stop crime" but to keep the local Punishment Industry supplied with victims. When the Romans ran out of criminals to feed to the lions, they scoured the world for edible prisoners of war. The Athenians used to designate some poor vagrant every year, drive him out of town, and subject him to a ritual stoning-to-death.

We think of ourselves as far more enlightened because our victims must be genuine criminals as certified by a court of law. The only exception is in the case of death-row inmates who turn out, at the very last moment, not to be guilty at all. In some cases the courts have ruled that they should fry anyway—because the facilities are ready and waiting and everyone is in the mood.

Other than that, we are restricted to criminals, as the word is generally defined, and the supply is by no means unlimited. One line of criminological reasoning, which might be called the "liberal" theory, holds that there is nothing wrong with our present approach to maintaining the crime supply. Just take a quarter of the child population, raise them in desperate poverty (with racial discrimination thrown in where applicable), and subject them to commercials, night and day, advising that life without one-hundred-dollar footwear is not worth living. As an added measure, make sure none of the available jobs pay more than about five dollars an hour, and presto—little muggers are born, and in numbers sufficient to stock the Punishment Industry for years to come!

Conservatives naturally question the liberal theory. They point to the occasional person who grows up poor and virtuous, or, alternatively, affluent and twisted. Deprivation and temptation are not enough, they say—a good supply of crime requires technology too. Hence the Republicans' understandable reluctance to get behind gun control. Why make it even marginally more difficult for a teenager to get his hands on a gun just as we are about to beef up the Punishment Industry with ultra-tough new legislation? As even the National Rifle Association is too modest to point out, there is no way we would lead the world in the business of crime and punishment if it were not for our wide-open supply of guns.

The other tried-and-true approach is to simply broaden the definition of crime. This is the function of drug prohibition. A few decades ago, a person who smoked marijuana was a degenerate rake or a dashing bohemian, depending on your point of view. Now he or she is a criminal, qualifying for years in the slammer. Some states have gone further, making possession of rolling papers an equally dastardly crime. Similarly the "crime" of graffiti writing could be broadened to include possession of a Magic Marker, or crossing state lines with intent to buy one. The possibilities are endless once you realize that there is no crime, no matter how seemingly minor, that cannot be federalized, subjected to mandatory minimum sentencing, or transformed into a capital offense.

But a growing number of experts, including many criminal judges, assure us that there is nothing to worry about. No matter how fiercely Draconian it becomes, the Punishment

Industry will never diminish the supply of crime. On the contrary, there is evidence that a few years in the pen serves to season a criminal and make him more productive at his work. So as long as we do nothing to disturb the marvelous synergy of poverty and temptation, guns on the street and gun-fun on the tube, the supply of crime will never fall below the widespread demand for punishment.

Or we could decide, all of us law-abiding citizens, to cut off crime at the source, where poverty intersects with weaponry, and to satisfy the public appetite for cruelty with something other than the Punishment Industry. Bearbaiting has been proposed; also cockfighting and the public torment of stray dogs.

[1994]

Why Do They

Keep Coming?

There's been a bit of understandable griping about all the attention murders get when the murderees are British or German. Americans don't even rate the local news unless their heads are left impaled on parking meters and their flesh is marketed as cutlets, but let some tourist get dispatched by a clean shot through the temple and suddenly we've got a "crime wave." No one is asking the obvious questions: Why do they come? And why, when it should be clear as a bell they're not wanted here, do they keep on coming?

Surely everyone in the world knows that Americans' love for immigrants is exceeded only by that of the native-born residents of Rostock, Germany—famed hot spot of anti-immigrant terrorism—and what is a tourist if not a short-lived version of an immigrant? They're all freeloaders in their own ways: The immigrants come here to enjoy our munificent welfare system and perhaps take in some cosmetic surgery on the Medicaid plan. And the tourists, for their part, saunter over completely unarmed, expecting us locals to protect them.

In fact everyone knows that the immigrants are a lot easier to take than the tourists. The immigrants pretty much stick low to the ground, trying to dodge the various vigilante groups.

In a restaurant you'll never find a Salvadoran immigrant, for example, working as maître d'. No, they prefer to wash dishes in the kitchen, sly fellows that they are, where they can remain safely out of sight. Tourists are a whole different matter, as any genuine native can tell you. They snatch the best tables, the ones overlooking the salad bar, where they do gross things like spreading catsup on pizza. Or they smoke in nonsmoking areas, lighting their Gauloises with twenty-dollar bills and kicking the locals when they scramble on the floor for the ashes.

The way the foreign press sees it, Americans, and especially Floridians, just have too many guns. But let's look at the actual facts. The poor tourist who was nearly incinerated in Tampa—an African American from New York who had the oxymoronic idea, for a man of his race, of a "southern vacation"—was not set on fire with a gun. When you count up all the torchings, bludgeonings, and attacks by trained alligators, you will find that guns have only a modest role to play in our vast tourist-dispatching industry.

The real issue, though, is why foreign tourists come to Florida at all when they could be tanning right now on the lovely beaches of Oslo or Reykjavík? What is the possible attraction? We have Jacksonville, for example, a place so deeply boring that the residents used to entertain themselves by standing on the overpasses and raining bullets down on the southbound lanes. Or there's Miami's South Beach, where you can see the same people you might otherwise find shopping in Milan or Munich, only naked and thoroughly stoned.

Then there's Orlando—a place where five-foot-high versions of Minnie Mouse stalk the public airport, embracing unwary travelers at random. Supposedly, children love Walt Disney World, but most children have no prior experience of fascism, and tend to go away thinking it's just a nice way to spend time with mice.

Or, finally, at the end of the line, there's Key West. Once

a soulful, run-down place inhabited by fugitives and novelists coping with alcoholic impairments, Key West is busily being redone as a vast open public latrine. On famed Duval Street, where the schoolboy vomit flows freely of a Saturday night, there's now a Ripley's Believe-It-or-Not and a topless hamburger franchise under construction. If you want a beach, it's best to bring your own sand—and some sandwiches wouldn't hurt either, since the local cuisine centers on the, sadly, not-yet-extinct conch.

All right, our ancestors were tourists too. But, in hundreds of years, we've managed to work the tourism gene out of our systems. We've learned to stay home, behind our alarm systems and window bars, venturing out only when the ammunition runs low. So come if you must, but don't expect us to cover you if you go outdoors.

[1993]

Tired and Out of

Compassion

Princess Di is going around with tear-filled eyes, we read, and making her usual delicate references to the loo. Ordinarily, when any celebrity has a problem—a bad-hair day or charges of multiple molestation—we crumple in sympathetic pain. But the only thing filling our eyes at this point is the dull glaze of numbed disbelief. Get a job, Di—anything—just leave us alone.

This churlishness sets in every year at about the same time, just as the baby Jesus makes his annual appearance at the mall. The media call it "compassion fatigue," which shows that it comes not from hard-heartedness but from caring far too much. All year long we strain those compassion muscles— pumping and panting and lifting—until—snap!—they can bear it no more. The thick, creamy milk of human compassion gets replaced by a bilious yellow phlegmlike fluid. "Enough," we say to the suffering world. "Let us shop and eat in peace!"

Take AIDS, for example, which ranks just behind Princess Di in the media's misery list. AIDS was isolated as a major cause of compassion fatigue years ago, but, incredibly enough, nothing has been done to stop it. Yes, it's terrible to have AIDS, but AIDS-compassion deserves sympathy too. It isn't easy to pin those little red ribbons to one's lapel, risking a pinprick to the fingertip and God knows what microbial incursions. Plus it's the people-without-AIDS who must single-handedly hold up the blood donation industry, and Liza Minelli never does a benefit for them.

Or there are the homeless. A couple of years ago, they were pinpointed as a leading cause of compassion fatigue. It's gone way beyond that now, all the way to compassion collapse. We dodge them on the street, which is exhausting enough, what with all the agile side steps and elbow action that's required to clear a path through midtown Manhattan. In addition, we pay good money in taxes to have their shanties and temporary shelters bulldozed down, thus helping the homeless face up to the full gravity of their situation instead of wallowing around in denial.

The same could be said for the poor as a group. They used up their compassion allotment decades ago, but insisted on sticking around. Our sympathies should now be reserved for those heroic policy wonks who toil night and day trying to figure out the quickest way to abolish the dole.

Salman Rushdie is another cause of full-body compassion depletion. Turn on the television, and he's always there, telling some auditorium full of people about the heart-wrenching problems of a life lived in total seclusion. What is it with these *fatwah* guys, one has to wonder—can't they get a copy of Rushdie's schedule from his publicist, just like anyone else? Eventually pity turns to its opposite, which is envy, for what writer has not dreamed of enjoying global fame while his publishers get picked off one by one?

Bosnia could be mentioned, except that the very word causes heads to pitch forward and tongues to loll in the final stages of compassion prostration. We don't mind a place when it's just a "hot spot," enlivening the news with fresh gore. But let it evolve beyond "hot spot" to "basket case," like Haiti or even

Liberia, and we understandably begin to tire. Somalia, for example, has just about drained the tear ducts dry, and now one cannot even think of the people over there—the poor U.N. fellows, that is, huddled in their barracks, persecuted by the nasty natives—without uttering a weary ho hum.

So maybe it's time to spare some compassion for the compassion-fatigued. Instead of stigmatizing them as "Scrooges" and "mean-spirited wretches," we need to realize they are no different from us. They have just cared more, felt more, perhaps even cried more—and now they are paying the price. They need rest, as we all know, plentiful fluids, and complete freedom from irritating or disturbing thoughts. A special ribbon color should be designated to indicate solidarity with the compassion-fatigued, and Princess Di—that lady of a thousand inscrutable sorrows—might want to lead the fund-raising effort.

[1993]

We're Number One!

The school board of Lake County, Florida, has ruled that students must be taught that American culture is superior to all other "foreign or historic cultures." Naturally, the multiculturalist symps are denouncing this edict as a species of mindless patriotism. They do not seem to realize that *mindless* patriotism consists of loving some country—Estonia, say, or Uruguay—just because you happen to reside in it, and without regard to its manifest inferiority vis-à-vis others. But what could be a more rational, clear-headed form of patriotism than to love a country which is, objectively speaking, superior to all other nations?

Interestingly, none of the school board's critics dares assert that America is *not* best. Most objections to the new curriculum, like columnist A. M. Rosenthal's in *The New York Times*, lead with the assertion that America is indeed the best, but nevertheless advise against telling the students this. You might offend some of the more multicultural kids, or make the blue-eyed white ones—few of whom can spell the plural of "country" anyway—even more sluggish and smug than they already are.

But why not approach the whole issue scientifically? Is the

United States really number one, or perhaps only number 17 or 93? Because if the United States can be proved to be number one, then this fact should be taught not only in Lake County but in schools across the globe. Surely no one is suggesting that truth is "relative"—say, to where you are standing at the moment—and that the bestness of America applies only in Lake County, Florida. And think how the study of geography will be simplified when all the world's nations can be ranked—from one to 200, or whatever it is—and students will be able to safely ignore all those below the top ten.

There is no shortage, of course, of anecdotal evidence establishing America as number one. Any American who ventures abroad—by, for example, boarding the wrong plane for Paris, Texas, or Naples, Florida—returns with horrifying tales of intestinal upsets and cabs driven by demonic deaf-mutes. Possibly some of the Lake County school-board members have themselves experienced the inferiority of alternative cultures: the natives' strained and desperate attempts to communicate in incomprehensible languages; the pathetic renditions of basic foodstuffs, such as pizza and burger with fries; the scratchy, unreliable toilet paper.

These shortcomings would be particularly vivid to anyone coming from Lake County, which is located only a few miles from Orlando—the veritable Athens of American culture—home of Epcot Center, Disney World, various snake and parrot worlds, and (when last I visited) Denture World.

But far more objective evidence lies at hand, in a book entitled *We're Number One: Where America Stands—and Falls—in the New World Order,* by Andrew L. Shapiro (1992). In this thoughtful, thoroughly footnoted volume, we learn that America is indeed number one, by dozens of measures.

Take "family values," which is one of the areas of national superiority proudly claimed by the Lake County school board. True enough, America leads the world in the number of people who marry and say they "believe in" marriage. We also have the highest divorce rate and are clearly "best"—at least until Rwanda came along—at the murder of children. So, yes, we do value the family, though perhaps not its particular members.

We are also number one in deaths by gun, which puts us well ahead of those backward nations where deaths are still being accomplished with crude bladed instruments like machetes.

Or take "free enterprise," another area of superiority the school board has cited. We are number one in the number of billionaires, also in the number of homeless people—showing that "free enterprise" is, indeed, at its reckless, anomic best right here in the U.S.A.

But why bother with such tedious proofs? We're also number one in the percentage of teenagers "who *don't* think science is useful in everyday life" and in the number of people who believe that "more respect for authority would be a good thing." So if the school board says we're number one, there's really nothing more to say.

[1994]

Onward, Christian Lite!

As it approaches the estimable age of 2000, the Judeo-Christian ethic seems to be going all soft and senile. A noisily Christian portion of the Virginia electorate was prepared to send a former felon to the Senate on the grounds that he never cheated on his wife. Former philanderer Ted Kennedy was almost unseated by an otherwise clean-living millionaire union-buster. In Haiti, born-again ex-president Jimmy Carter invited torture-master Raoul Cédras to teach Sunday school, apparently because his wife is slender and his shirts well pressed. Everywhere, private virtue—or the successful simulation of it—seems to count more than public morality, and material wealth more than anything else. In the new, mellowed-out version of the old-time ethic, you can lie, steal, and trample on the poor—so long as you keep those zippers zipped.

True enough, the Bible has a great deal to say on the subject of zippers, or their A.D. 1 equivalent. Thou shalt not lust after your neighbor's wife or livestock. Thou shalt not spill the seed that was intended for your brother's widow. Thou shalt not divorce, or, better yet, even marry in the first place, but wander around single and celibate, spreading the word.

This is stern stuff, and an abiding challenge to the wayward flesh. But this is the easy part. The hard part is the social side of the Judeo-Christian ethic, meaning not how you treat the spouse and kids but how you conduct yourself in the world beyond the bedroom and the den. We don't hear about it so much since the word "Christian" began its oxymoronic partnership with the smug word "right," but Scripture demands unstinting charity, if not all-out dedication to the poor.

Recall Jesus' encounter with the wealthy young fellow who claimed exemplary zeal in the zipper department. He had followed the Ten Commandments to the letter, so was he entitled now to eternal life? No was the unambiguous answer; the next step was to "go and sell that thou hast, and give to the poor." Jesus then offered his famous observation on camels and needles and how futile it is for rich folks to try to wriggle their way into heaven.

All right, maybe camels were smaller then and needles a lot more wide-eyed. But the message is reiterated in passage after passage, and not only in the politically suspect New Testament, where socialists have always found solace. Ezekiel explains that the Sodomites' sin was that they had "pride, fullness of bread, and abundance of idleness," but did not "strengthen the hand of the poor and needy" (16:49)—quite apart from any "sodomy." Amos addresses the rich people of Bashan, "which oppress the poor, which crush the needy," and thunders that "the days shall come upon you, that he will take you away with hooks, and your posterity with fishhooks" (4:1–2) (which puts even "necklacing" in a new perspective).

So, to echo some of our self-righteously Christian spokesmen, how far we have strayed from the narrow path prescribed by the prophets! A sizable portion of the electorate, probably no less Judeo-Christian than anyone else, stands ready to let the richer candidate buy their votes, on the theory that the rich cannot be bought themselves. In the case of Michael

Huffington in California or Ross Perot in 1992, piles of earthly treasure were proffered, with a straight face, as proof of one's ability to lead. But who can fault our lucre-crazed political culture when even the televangelists promise financial well-being, i.e., "fullness of bread" as the reward for supposedly Christian virtue?

The poor themselves, in a stunning inversion of Scripture, have taken the place of the demons and Pharisees. Well-fed intellectuals trip over one another in their eagerness to castigate the down-and-out as muggers, sluts, dope fiends, and even— in the case of Richard J. Herrnstein and Charles Murray in their new book, *The Bell Curve*—retards and morons. No political candidate dares step up on a podium without promising to execute, imprison, and snatch alms from the hands of the "underclass." Blessed are those that find fault with the poor, one might imagine the Bible saying, for they shall inherit the Senate.

In the midst of this profound moral confusion, the Haiti crisis came like a test from on high. Here were good and evil laid out in black and white, or, rather, black and creamy mulatto: the pastel luxury of Pétionville versus the dark, bottomless misery of the shantytowns. And in Jean-Bertrand Aristide, here was as Christ-like a figure as ever headed a state: devout, dedicated to the poor, and celibate on top of all that. Yet from Clinton's flip-flops to Carter's flirtation with Cédras, we dithered shamefully. Even after the troops had arrived— and with less prior dithering, no troops would ever have been necessary—it was unclear for days whether they were there to protect the rich and their "attachés" from the poor, or the poor from their well-heeled tormentors.

Now, of course, Scripture is open to interpretation; ethics do change with the times. We don't prohibit shellfish anymore, or appease the deity with slaughtered rams. But there's something suspect about a brand of Judeo-Christianity that can get all het up about the spilling of seed while gliding right past the Sermon on the Mount. We seem to have chosen the easy path, the one that comforts the already comfortable and harangues the already hard-pressed. We're the post-Judeo-Christian generation, and Christian Right turns out to mean Christian Lite.

[1994]

Kicking the Big One

An evil grips America, a life-sapping drug-related habit. It beclouds reason and corrodes the spirit. It undermines authority and nourishes a low-minded culture of winks and smirks. It's the habit of drug prohibition, and it's quietly siphoning off the resources that might be better used for drug treatment or prevention. Numerous authorities have tried to warn us, including, most recently, the surgeon general, but she got brushed off like a piece of lint. After all, drug prohibition is right up there with heroin and nicotine among the habits that are hell to kick.

Admittedly, legalization wouldn't be problem-free either. Americans have a peculiarly voracious appetite for drugs, and probably no one should weigh into the debate who hasn't seen a friend or loved one hollowed out by cocaine or reduced to selling used appliances on the street. But if drugs take a ghastly toll, drug prohibition has proved itself, year after year, to be an even more debilitating social toxin.

Consider the moral effects of marijuana prohibition. After booze and NyQuil, pot is probably America's No. 1 drug of choice—a transient, introspective high that can cure nausea or make the evening sitcoms look like devastating wit. An estimated 40 million Americans have tried it at some point, from Ivy League law professors to country-and-western singers. Yet in some states, possession of a few grams can get you put away for years—even if it was a gift you were taking to your dying mother in the chemotherapy ward.

What does it do to one's immortal soul to puff, and wink, and look away while about 100,000 other Americans remain locked up for doing the exact same thing? Marijuana prohibition establishes a minimum baseline level of cultural dishonesty that we can never rise above: The president "didn't inhale," heh heh. It's okay to drink till you puke, but you mustn't ever smoke the vile weed, heh heh. One of the hardest things a parent can ever tell a bright and questioning teenager—after all the relevant sermonizing, of course—is, Well, just don't get caught.

But the prohibition of cocaine and heroin may be more corrosive still. Here's where organized crime comes in, the cartels and kingpins and Crips and Bloods. These are the principal beneficiaries of drug prohibition; without it, they'd be reduced to three-card monte and numbers scams. Legitimate entrepreneurs must sigh and shake their heads in envy: if only the government would so willingly collude with them—banning some substance like Wheat Chex, for example, so that it could be marketed for hundreds of dollars per ounce.

Yes, legal drugs, even if heavily taxed and extensively regulated, will no doubt be cheaper than illegal ones, which could mean more people sampling them out of curiosity. But this danger has to be weighed against the insidious marketing dynamic of illegal drugs, whose wildly inflated prices compel the low-income user to become a pusher and recruiter of new users. The only way we could match the current street-level sales effort would be to advertise cocaine on MTV.

Drugs can kill, of course. But drug prohibition kills, too.

In Washington, D.C., an estimated 80 percent of homicides are drug-related, meaning drug prohibition–related. It's gunshot wounds that fill our urban emergency rooms, not O.D.'s and bad trips. Then there's the perverse financial logic of prohibition. The billions we spend a year on drug-related law enforcement represents money not spent on improving schools and rebuilding neighborhoods. Those who can't hope for the lasting highs of achievement and self-respect are all too often condemned to crack.

So why don't we kick the prohibition habit? Is it high-minded puritanism that holds us back, or run-of-the-mill political cowardice? Or maybe it's time to admit that we cling to prohibition for the same reason we cling to so many other self-destructive habits—because we like the way they make us feel. Prohibition, for example, tends to make its advocates feel powerfully righteous, and militant righteousness has effects not unlike some demon mix of liquor and amphetamines: the eyes bulge, the veins distend, the voice begins to bray.

But the most seductive thing about prohibition is that it keeps us from having to confront all the other little addictions that get us through the day. It's the NutraSweet in the coffee we use to wash down the chocolate mousse; a dad's "just say no" commandments borne on martini-scented breath. "Don't do drugs," a Members Only ad advises. "Do clothes." Well, why "do" anything? Why not live more lightly, without compulsions of any kind? Then there's TV, the addiction whose name we can hardly speak—the poor man's virtual reality, the substance-free citizen's 24-hour-a-day hallucinatory trip. No bleary-eyed tube addict, emerging from weekend-long catatonia, has the right to inveigh against "drugs."

When cornered, the prohibition addict has one last line of defense. We can't surrender in this war, he or she insists, because we'd be sending the "wrong message." But the message we're sending now is this: Look, kids, we know prohibition doesn't work, that it's cruel and costs so much we don't have anything left over with which to fight the social causes of addiction or treat the addicts, but hey, it feels good, so we're going to keep right on doing it. To which the appropriate response is, of course, Heh heh.

We don't have to quit cold turkey. We could start with marijuana, then ease up on cocaine and heroin possession, concentrating law enforcement on the big-time pushers. Take it slowly, see how it feels . . . One day at a time.

[1994]

TRAMPLING

ON THE

DOWN-AND-OUT

Welfare:

A White Secret

Come on, my fellow white folks, we have something to confess. No, nothing to do with age spots or those indoor-tanning creams we use to get us through the winter without looking like the final stages of TB. Nor am I talking about the fact that we all go home and practice funky dance moves behind drawn shades. Out with it, friends, the biggest secret known to whites since the invention of powdered rouge: welfare is a white program. Yep. At least it's no more black than Vanilla Ice is a fair rendition of classic urban rap.

The numbers go like this: 61 percent of the population receiving welfare, listed as "means-tested cash assistance" by the Census Bureau, is identified as white (a category that includes most hispanics), while only 33 percent is identified as black. These numbers notwithstanding, the Republican version of "political correctness" has given us "welfare cheat" as a new term for African American since the early days of Ronald Reagan. Yet if the Lakers were 61 percent white and on a winning streak, would we be calling them a "black team"?

Wait a minute, I can hear my neighbors say; we're not as slow at math as the Asian Americans like to think. There's still a glaring disproportion there. African Americans are only

12 percent of the population as a whole, at least according to the census count, yet they're 33 percent of the welfare population—surely evidence of a shocking addiction to the dole.

But we're forgetting something. Welfare is a program for poor people, very poor people. African Americans are three times as likely as whites to fall below the poverty level and hence to have a chance of qualifying for welfare benefits. If we look at the kind of persons most likely to be eligible— single mothers living in poverty with children under eighteen to support—we find little difference in welfare participation by race: 74.6 percent of African Americans in such dire straits are on welfare, compared with 64.5 percent of the poor white single moms.

That's still a difference, but not enough to imply some congenital appetite for a free lunch on the part of the African-derived. In fact, two explanations readily suggest themselves: First, just as blacks are disproportionately likely to be poor, they are disproportionately likely to find themselves among the poorest of the poor, where welfare eligibility arises. Second, the black poor are more likely than their white counterparts to live in cities, and hence to have a chance of making their way to the welfare office. Correct for those two differences, and you won't find an excess of African Americans fitting the stereotype of the sluttish welfare queen who breeds for profit.

So why are they so poor? I can see my neighbor asking as visions of feckless idlers dance before his narrowed eyes. Ah, that is a question white folks would do well to ponder. Consider, for a start, that African Americans are more likely to be disabled (illness being a famous consequence of poverty) or unemployed (in the sense of actively seeking work) and far less likely to earn wages that would lift them out of the welfare-eligibility range.

As for the high proportion of black families headed by single women (44 percent, compared with 13 percent for whites): many deep sociohistoric reasons could be adduced, but none of them is welfare. A number of respected studies refute the Reagan-era myth that a few hundred a month in welfare payments is a sufficient incentive to chuck one's husband or get pregnant while in high school. If it were, states with relatively high welfare payments—say, about $500 a month per family—would have higher rates of out-of-wedlock births than states like Louisiana and Mississippi, which expect a welfare family to get by on $200 a month or less. But this is not the case.

So our confession stands: white folks have been gobbling up the welfare budget while blaming someone else. But it's worse than that. If we look at Social Security, which is another form of welfare, although it is often mistaken for an individual insurance program, then whites are the ones who are crowding the trough. We receive almost twice as much per capita, for an aggregate advantage to our race of $10 billion a year—much more than the $3.9 billion advantage African Americans gain from their disproportionate share of welfare. One sad reason: whites live an average of six years longer than African Americans, meaning that young black workers help subsidize a huge and growing "overclass" of white retirees.

But I do not see our confession bringing much relief. There's a reason for resentment, though it has more to do with class than with race. White people are poor, too, and in numbers far exceeding any of our more generously pigmented social groups. And poverty as defined by the government is a vast underestimation of the economic terror that persists at incomes—such as $20,000 or even $40,000 and above—that we like to think of as middle class.

The problem is not that welfare is too generous to blacks but that social welfare in general is too stingy to all concerned. Naturally, whites in the swelling "near poor" category resent the notion of whole races supposedly frolicking at their expense. Whites, near poor and middle class, need help too—as do the many African Americans, Hispanics, and "others" who do not qualify for aid but need it nonetheless.

So we white folks have a choice. We can keep pretending that welfare is a black program and a scheme for transferring our earnings to the pockets of shiftless, dark-skinned people. Or we can clear our throats, blush prettily, and admit that we are hurting too—for cash assistance when we're down and out, for health insurance, for college aid and all the rest.

Racial scapegoating has its charms, I will admit: the surge of righteous anger, even the fun—for those inclined—of wearing sheets and burning crosses. But there are better, nobler sources of white pride, it seems to me. Remember, whatever they say about our music or our taste in clothes, only we can truly, deeply blush.

[1991]

S-M as Public Policy

Welfare may turn out to be the domestic equivalent of Saddam Hussein. Already, leading pundits have declared it to be a crucial test of Bill Clinton's manhood: Will he be tough enough to crack down on those lazy sluts who insist on living off government funds, as legions of tweed-jacketed policy wonks demand? Or will he cave in to the welfare wimps—such as, presumably, Donna Shalala—with their squeamish aversion to mass starvation? Meanwhile, no one seems to have noticed that there is an ingenious, low-cost solution that has the potential to please both sides: allow welfare recipients to continue to collect their miserly checks, but require that they submit, periodically, to public floggings.

Distasteful? Perhaps, but punishment has become a major cultural theme of our time. Consider Madonna's oeuvre, with its emphasis on bondage and whips. Or listen to the nation's leading pundits, as they jump up and down, much like masochists at a sex orgy, demanding that Clinton give us "pain and sacrifice!" On account of the deficit, the reasoning goes, what America needs now is a good sound "spankie." And who better to take the punishment than a social group that has no money, no friends in high places, and not a speck of political clout?

Everyone from neoliberal to neoconservative agrees that something must be done. It's not so much the money (welfare consumes only one percent of the federal budget) as the principle of the thing. In dozens of universities and think tanks, scholarly males grow apoplectic at the thought of fifteen-year-olds using pregnancy to get their first rent-free studio apartments. Hence the widespread excitement over Clinton's campaign proposal to limit welfare to two years, during which the recipients will be treated to job training and child care, and after which they will have to scavenge for food as they may.

But a program of welfare plus floggings makes far more sense in every way. First, it will be no less effective at curing poverty than any amount of job training and forced work experience. For decades now, welfare recipients have been subjected to dozens of workfare and work-incentive programs. They have been taught how to dress for job interviews, how to find their way through the want ads, how to process words and tote up numbers. The effects, as now even the most ardent welfare hawks acknowledge, have been negligible: only minuscule gains in income and an inevitable drift back to the welfare rolls. This is not because welfare recipients are incorrigibly lazy. In a labor market where 18 percent of workers already toil full-time, year-round, to earn less than poverty-level wages, there are few vacant jobs that offer a living wage, especially to unskilled females with child-care problems.

Second, the welfare-plus-floggings program will be far cheaper than any work program so far devised. The conservative estimate is that it would cost $50 billion a year to ready the welfare population for the labor market—roughly twice what is spent on welfare in its present form—and that about half of this sum will be spent on child care. So what will really be accomplished by getting welfare recipients trained and out of their houses? The ten million children on welfare, who are now cared for by their mothers at home, will instead be cared for by other poor women called child-care workers—while the mothers take up data entry and burger flipping. The net result, needless to say, will be a surge of commuting among the preschool set.

But the real beauty of the welfare-plus-floggings approach is that it will provide an outlet for the punitive rage now directed at the down-and-out. In a curious inversion of the Sermon on the Mount, no social group attracts more ire than the vaguely termed "underclass." The need to punish the poor is, of course, already built into the present welfare system, which insists that recipients travel from one government office to another, usually with children in tow, and submit to intimate investigations of their finances, sleeping arrangements, and housekeeping habits. Often this bureaucratic harassment reaches fiendish proportions, driving many poor women from the dole. But imagine the much more vivid effect that could be achieved by the actual drawing of blood!

Madonna aside, sadomasochism is entirely consistent with recent political trends. For twelve years now, we've had presidents who have understood the primary function of government to be punishment in one form or another. All available funds have been channeled into the military, which rushes about the world like a schoolmistress armed with a birch rod. Bad countries—like Grenada, Panama, Libya, Iraq—are soundly whipped and sent to stand in their corners. Why, even as he was dragged from the Oval Office, George Bush managed to lash out once again at Saddam—with a "spanking," as *Time* magazine so insightfully put it.

Domestically, too, the punishment theme has been strictly adhered to. While all other domestic functions of government have withered away, the prison system has expanded to the point where the United States is second only to Russia in the percentage of its citizens incarcerated. For poor males, we have prison; for poor females, welfare—and there's no reason why one sex's punishment should be any less onerous than the other's.

It's not that the welfare recipients have done anything wrong. On the contrary, they've been neglected by underfunded schools; abused, in many cases, by husbands and boyfriends; and left to fend for their children in trailer camps or cities that resemble Mogadishu.

But we all know that "welfare reform" means, in plain English, that someone has got to be punished. Programs that throw women off welfare into unemployment or poverty-level jobs will punish, ultimately, their children. Hence the brilliance of the flogging approach: it will make the hawks and the wonks feel much better—without starving a single child.

[1993]

How Labor's Love

Was Lost

There is something awkward and embarrassing about Labor Day. Here it is: a major national holiday, our one and only chance to celebrate, or at least try to recall, the working person, yet no one thinks to send their loved ones Labor Day cards. There is no talk of the "spirit of Labor Day," no keen anticipation among the children on Labor Day Eve. The only certified Labor Day events are the tedious annual op-ed pieces entitled "Remember the Labor Movement?" and the grilling of millions of turkey dogs. Because the sad truth, we all know, is that American labor—far from being the muscular sine qua non of industrial might—has become an object of horror and revulsion.

We should have realized this years ago when companies first started relocating, as fast as they could pack up their work stations and tools, in faraway lands where no American worker was ever likely to venture. First they took out the assembly lines and shipped them to Mexico and Malaysia. Then they eliminated the word-processing pools, sending the clerical work by modem to workers in Jamaica. That was the point when American workers should have stood up as one and demanded: "Hey, what's the matter with *us*? Is it unsightly facial hair or some other easily correctable problem of personal hygiene?"

But no, American labor just didn't take the hint. Ordinarily, when people cough lightly and move away at one's approach, one learns to keep to oneself. But American labor kept whining and pleading: "Jobs! Give us jobs! Please let us come and help out in any way we can! We'll learn computer skills, we'll dress in unsightly green uniforms, we'll grovel and fawn!"

The bosses just rolled their eyes, gagging slightly, and began to shut down the plants one by one. "Downsizing" they called it, so no one's feelings would be hurt. "Small is beautiful," they mumbled at Kodak and GM and Boeing as they handed out pink slips by the tens of thousands. But, in fact, they just couldn't get out to the third world fast enough, and the corporate consensus seems to be: if you need American workers to make something, it's better to make nothing at all.

Oh, there've been various face-saving explanations offered along the way. "American workers are just too expensive" was the standard argument for years: why pay dollars per hour in Detroit when you can pay dollars per day in Taiwan or Tijuana? But it's been a long time since American workers were paid more than it costs to buy Styrofoam packing material and ship a plant south of the border. In fact, one of the many little ways management has tried to discourage American workers from showing up at the factory gates morning after morning was by taking away their health insurance and much of their pay. When hourly wages dipped lower than the tip due a waiter at an executive lunch—which happened in about 1983—the bosses figured the employees would just walk off the job in a snit.

If cost is not the problem, then it must be some unpleasant personal attribute of the American workforce that is driving the employers away. This is not as farfetched as it may at first seem. In the United States today, the average CEO earns 85 times as much as the average worker. For the average CEO, a factory full of $7-an-hour people represents the kind of neighborhood that is best avoided without an armed escort tagging along. Why expose yourself unnecessarily to large numbers of surly, low-income types?

Nor can conflicting standards of personal hygiene be entirely ruled out. At an 85-to-1 earnings ratio, we are dealing with the kind of gap that separated Marie Antoinette from the louse-ridden peasants that peopled her realm. She would hardly have been expected to mingle with them willingly, day after day, out of a simple desire to keep them employed.

When will American workers realize they are no longer wanted? That their wages are calculated insults, designed, in fact, to drive them away? The appropriate response to rejection is not to march around pathetically demanding "Jobs!" but to come up with a wholly new strategy for making a living. Here the criminal underclass may be in the vanguard, with their straightforward demands for money without the ghastly entanglement of the employer-employee relationship. And the finicky American boss-class will probably be relieved, in the end, to simply hand over their wallets and run.

[1993]

An Epidemic of

Munchausen's Syndrome

It's easy for Europeans to laugh at Americans for having no form of national health care—easy but cruel, like finding amusement in a palsy victim's efforts to tap-dance. There is a good reason why America can't have national health insurance, a medical reason in fact. No one wants to say it out loud for fear of causing a panic, but it is well known to all the expert advisers who helped Hillary Clinton prepare her health-reform proposal. The sad fact, revealed here for the first time in public, is that Americans are suffering from an epidemic of Munchausen's syndrome.

Of course, AIDS and breast cancer get all the attention, but it's Munchausen's that makes us unfit for national health care. Defined in the medical literature as "repeated fabrication of illness . . . by a person who wanders from hospital to hospital for treatment," Munchausen's was once an arcane diagnosis, better known to psychiatry than to medicine. Today, however, it sends millions of us out begging for shots, pills, X rays, anything—mole removals, cervical scrapings, little biopsies of this or that.

It wasn't always like this, the experts will tell you. Many years ago, before there were health-insurance companies, people used to pay for care themselves—"out of pocket," as the expression goes. Thus they thought twice about begging the doctor to throw in a hysterectomy or a heart transplant along with the annual physical. Munchausen's remained in check.

But things got more expensive in time, especially the complex, high-tech things that doctors use, like eight-cylinder sports cars and three-speed Jacuzzis and forty-foot yachts. In response, the great insurance companies arose, with the simple idea of helping out. Who could have guessed that the effect would be to unleash Munchausen's on an epidemic scale? Freed from the burden of payment on the spot, Americans went on an orgy of health-care consumption: Don't give me a refillable prescription, they would beg their doctors; let me come back every month for a new one! Or how about a CAT scan, they would plead, in that wonderful new CAT-scanning facility you own down the street? Or a sigmoidoscopy, please, just a quickie?

Hence the health-care crisis, at least according to the insurance industry's experts and their scores of close friends in Washington: Mass Munchausen's! Not to mention Munchausen's-by-proxy, in which neurotic moms drag their children in for excess throat cultures and perhaps a wee amputation. The insurance companies fought back in the only ways they knew: first they raised their premiums, eliminating all but the wealthy; then they quietly weeded out anyone with breast lumps or HIV or angina or any other telltale sign of incipient Munchausen's. Well, what were they to do? Insurance companies have stockholders who, as we know, are for the most part widows and orphans subsisting on their dividend checks.

Polls show that 70 percent of Americans—maddened by health insurers who refuse to insure anyone but the certifiably healthy—favor a Canadian-style system of national health insurance. The 1,500 private insurance companies would be replaced by a single, public-sector insurer, and everyone would be entitled to medical care whenever they needed it. But isn't this just what you'd expect from a population deep in the grip of Munchausen's? Give us a Canadian-style system, and eighty-year-olds will be demanding cesarean sections! Teenagers will insist on colostomies!

Hence the plan favored by the Clintons' cadre of experts. "Managed competition" would leave everything exactly as it is, except that a new entity—a health-insurance purchasing cooperative—would be layered on top like surgical dressing over a gangrenous wound. We'll have to purchase our health insurance through one of these cooperatives, which will in turn purchase it from one of the 1,500 private insurance companies, which will in turn attempt to force us into "managed care" plans in which one will have no choice of physicians and no opportunity to indulge in gluttonous medical consumption.

The public will not be happy with managed competition. Many will actually see their coverage decline, and, according to the Government Accounting Office, there will be no savings in public expenditures. But the point, we should recall, is not to solve the "health-care crisis." The point is to stem the scourge of Munchausen's.

[1993]

Real Babies,

Illegitimate Debates

If she's following the welfare reform debate, Anita Hill must be having posttraumatic flashbacks. Here we have a collection of important white males, including Bill Clinton, Daniel Moynihan, and Bill Bennett, scowling down on one small, scared female figure—embodied, in this case, in the Welfare Recipient. The women of the five million families on welfare are no more, and no less, representative of American womanhood than Anita Hill was. But the assault on welfare, like the Senate committee's interrogation of Professor Hill, is an implicit attack on the dignity and personhood of every woman, black or white, poor or posh.

Take first the universal, nearly unquestioned assumption that welfare mothers "don't work," and that the goal of reform is to get them out of their own kitchens and into those of, say, Burger King. Well, ladies, what have we been doing in our kitchens all these years if not some species of work? No one receives AFDC payments without having at least one child to feed, wash, dress, and pick up after, and the assumption of the welfare reformers seems to be that these activities are on a par with soap watching and bonbon consumption. In the conceptual framework which holds that welfare mothers "don't work," affluent married homemakers can't rank much higher than courtesans.

Churlish males have suspected for decades that homemaking is little more than a sinecure for the low-skilled and occupationally impaired. Of course, no husband dares look his wife in the eye—often bloodshot from sleep deprivation—and tell her that she "doesn't work." Yet somehow the insult is assumed to be forgivable when directed at the down-and-out.

The most pernicious feature of the current welfare debate though, from a feminine point of view, has to be the thriving new rhetoric of "illegitimacy." Until just a few months ago, the term "illegitimate," when applied to a human child, had more or less fallen from use and been replaced by the less pejorative "out-of-wedlock." The courts have been steadily erasing the ancient disadvantages of being born to unmarried parents. Feminists have insisted that every child is equally real and deserving, regardless of the circumstances of its conception.

Then Dan Quayle, followed by professional welfare-basher Charles Murray, decided that the old stigma against the out-of-wedlock was in urgent need of revival. What's the cause of poverty, crime, and general moral decay? Not laziness, according to the new conservative analysis, but sin. "Illegitimate" babies are clogging the welfare rolls, and welfare, perversely, is said to be an incentive for the production of more of them. According to one on-line database, the number of newspaper articles linking welfare and "illegitimacy" hovered at around 100 a year or less between 1990 and 1993, and then jumped to 157 for the first six months of 1994 alone.

In fact, "illegitimacy" has about as much to do with welfare as baldness does with Social Security expenditures. Women on welfare actually experience lower birthrates than other women, and numerous studies have established that welfare does *not* serve as an incentive to bear additional babies. Plus

if the welfare-bashers would look up from the fabled underclass, they'd see that out-of-wedlock births are increasing
throughout the industrial world and in all social classes—not
because of generous welfare policies but because of changing
mores and, in many instances, declining male wages. Recall
that Dan Quayle's original target wasn't some impecunious
pregnant teenager but the high-achieving Murphy Brown.

Now women may differ on whether extramarital sex is a
sin, punishable by perpetual scorn. But when the products of
such unions are restigmatized as "illegitimate," all women,
chaste or otherwise, are potentially on shaky ground. The
implication is that a mother can give birth, but only a father
can confer full membership in the human community, i.e.,
"legitimacy." A child that no man has stepped forth to
claim—either through marriage or later legal "legitimation"
procedures—becomes somehow less worthy and human. In
English common law, an out-of-wedlock child was *filius nul-
lius*, meaning child of no one. The kid was a bastard, and the
mother, being single and female, counted for nothing at all.

The immediate victims of the new welfare rhetoric will be
the children of poor single women. They're the ones who'll
have to face the restigmatization of "illegitimacy"—in the
playground, where it will really hurt. They're the ones who'll
come home to empty apartments while their mothers process
words and flip burgers. And, as dozens of disappointing
welfare-to-work programs have shown, the low-wage jobs usually available to welfare recipients are hardly a cure for poverty.
The net result of forcing welfare mothers to work will be a
further decline in wages for everyone—as millions of desperate
women flood the workforce—plus a surge of commuting
among the preschool set.

But the ultimate targets of the antiwelfare rhetoric are
women, and not just the poor. Going after upscale women
can still be a political faux pas, as Dan Quayle discovered.

But the Welfare Mother makes an ideal scapegoat for the imagined sins of womankind in general. She's officially manless, in defiance of the patriarchal norm, just like any brazen executive-class single-mother-by-choice. At the same time, she's irritatingly "dependent," like the old-fashioned, cookie-baking mom. But unlike her more upscale sisters, the welfare mom is too poor and despised to mount an effective defense. And unlike Anita Hill, she's never once, in the entire debate, been invited to speak.

[1994]

Honor to

the Working Stiffs

Put another wienie on the fire for the working class. It's time for the annual barbecue in honor of the people who slaughtered the pigs, and made the hot dog, and trucked it to market, and bagged it for you. The little guy and gal, that is, the working stiffs. They could use a little honor these days. At the rate blue-collar wages are falling, the United States is going to reinvent slavery in the next few decades, only without any of its nice, redeeming features, such as room and board.

A job is supposed to be a ticket to self-respect and social betterment—at least that's what the pols tell us when the poor start clamoring for their welfare checks. But conditions in the low-wage end of the workforce are beginning to look like what Engels found in nineteenth-century Manchester and later described as "immiseration." Within ten miles of my own suburban home, for example, there is a factory where (until they got a union contract a year ago) the workers slept in their cars and bathed in the ladies' room—because, at the minimum wage, housing was not an option. A few miles in the other direction, Salvadoran refugees report getting $125 in cash for sixty-hour weeks of heavy outdoor labor. For them, upward mobility would be a busboy's job at $2.90 an hour plus a cut of the tips.

Or I think of Jean-Paul, a Haitian-born janitor in one of the local schools. He's only a janitor at night. By day he works an eight-hour factory shift. On weekends he washes cars. That leaves eight hours a day, on average, for sleeping, eating, commuting, washing, and brooding, as Jean-Paul often does, on the meaning of his life.

These are not isolated, exotic cases. Nationwide, the fraction of the workforce earning poverty-level wages rose from 25.7 percent in 1979 to 31.5 percent in 1987. During the eighties, the average hourly earnings of all blue-collar workers fell by $1.68, and those who were earning the least to start with tended to lose the most. In what some sociologists call the "new working class"—which is disproportionately minorities and the young and female of all races—work may be a fine ingredient for an "ethic." But it doesn't really pay.

Ask a tweed-suited member of the better-paid classes what's gone wrong, and you'll get a lot of chin stroking about vast impersonal forces such as declining productivity and global competition. But real wages fell faster in the eighties than in the seventies, although productivity *rose* faster in the eighties. And theories of the global economy may explain a lot of things, but they don't make it any easier for a U.S. worker to live on third-world wages.

Or go to Washington, and you'll find an administration that loves the working class—as a concept anyway. George Bush favored pork cracklings, and was probably munching on that well-known proletarian treat as he nixed the bill that would have extended unemployment benefits. Bill Clinton got labor's vote, then forgot his promise to raise the minimum wage. Labor is like motherhood to most of our political leaders: a calling so fine and noble that it would be sullied by talk of vulgar, mundane things like pay.

Even unions aren't much help anymore. Union workers earn 30 percent more, on average, than their nonunion counterparts, but there aren't many union workers left. Only 16.1 percent of the workforce is organized, and that number is falling fast. Union leaders complain that it's hard to organize under a government that doesn't adequately enforce the rights of workers (to join a union, for example, without risking being fired). But the unions haven't exactly been exerting themselves: according to the Labor Research Association, the number of organizing drives keeps declining from year to year, and when unions do go to war, it's too often with each other. In 1990, for example, four major unions spent an estimated $40 to $50 million battling each other to represent Indiana state employees—as if they were the last nonunion workers left on earth.

This isn't just a "labor problem." It hurts us all when hard work doesn't pay, and I'm talking about insidious, creeping, moral damage. Conservatives like to cite that ancient Puritan teaching: He who does not work, neither should he eat. But the flip side of that stern motto should be written in the social contract, too: He who *does* work does deserve a decent break. No footnotes about productivity, no disclaimers about global competition, no fine print about the rights of stockholders and CEOs—just a guarantee that hard work will be rewarded with some baseline of comfort, nutrition, and dignity. This was the principle behind the minimum wage, even if it's much too low: that survival cannot be left entirely to market forces or employer whim.

Take that guarantee away and despair sets in, followed swiftly by cynicism and eventually maybe rage. For a man like Jean-Paul, it's the despair of knowing that his work, his energy, his *life*, that is, are valued at five dollars and change an hour, less than it costs him to pay for lunch. For his children, the response may well be cynicism. The message from the Bureau of Labor Statistics is clear: Don't bother with a job. Go on welfare if you can. Rob a convenience store. Open up a cocaine dealership. Jobs are for chumps.

We need a little less talk about the "work ethic" and a little more ethics in relation to work. The president could set an example by expending some political capital to pass the union-backed bill that would prohibit the use of strikebreakers and give workers a fighting chance. Employers might think twice about spending more on union-busting "consultants" than a pay raise would have cost. The unions ought to lead the way, not just with a few scattered organizing drives here and there but with something far more evangelical—a national crusade, let's say, drawing on churches, communities, and campus idealists. And what could be more American? The way to honor work, which we all claim to do, is, first of all, to pay for it.

[1991]

Fear of Easter

Ah, spring! The blizzards begin to abate. The gentle worms creep out of the soil to be pecked to death by robins. And it was in this season, we recall, that the baby Jesus underwent torture, burial, and resurrection. Inevitably, the question arises, What if He came back? For *The New York Times* reports that TV talk-lord Larry King is already planning to book Him, should the Second Coming coincide with prime time, and is hoping to make Him squirm with queries such as, Are You really the product of a virgin birth?

Surely there has never been a time when His faithful minions, few as they are, were under more vicious attack. Throughout the nation, upscale neighborhoods are mobilizing to prevent the construction of churches—because of the parking problem, of course, and the churches' repulsive tendency to attract the hungry and homeless to their occasional feeding programs. "Churches are no longer seen as assets to the community," the Reverend Thomas Starnes is quoted as saying. "Now it's 'There goes the neighborhood.' "

Along the same lines, the New York City subways have posted notices advising against the giving of alms. Except for a few religious fanatics and possible candidates for crucifixion, no one dares risk the wrath of their fellow passengers by tossing change into a trembling palm. The beggars now slither by downcast, dodging the spittle of the better-off.

Or we learn of the death of the Reverend Accelynne Williams, a seventy-five-year-old scriptural scholar, when a police SWAT team in Boston precipitated a fatal heart attack by breaking down his door, chasing him around his apartment, and handcuffing him without explanation. It was a drug raid of course, and, as often happens, the SWAT fellows had the wrong place. An understandable mistake, my own neighbors say, since the reverend had the depravity to live in a drug-infested zone and was, in addition, black.

We should also note the tornado that leveled an Alabama church in the middle of a Palm Sunday service, killing sixteen, including the pastor's four-year-old daughter. More appalling mischief from the Tormentor of Job, Williams might have concluded. Then you learn that the pastor was a woman, so that the entire proceedings constituted a form of devil worship—at least from the point of view of those Christians who see the ordained penis as a vital link, a connecting rod so to speak, to our Heavenly Father above.

Cynics delight in saying that Jesus would never make it in the modern capitalist world, where usury is the very elixir of life. We have tough laws against vagrancy now, not to mention consorting with prostitutes. The hair would be another problem, as would the wearing of skirts.

But the cynics exaggerate, as usual. First, there is no question that the baby Jesus could be born today, just as He was two millennia ago. If Mary attempted to find an abortion in the United States, she would wander from county to county, 83 percent of which offer no abortion services at all. Once she found a suitable facility, she might be forced to sit out a legally prescribed twenty-four-hour waiting period somewhere in a local manger, or perhaps come up with parental consent.

Then, when they discovered that the baby's grandfather and dad were one and the same, Mary would be dragged from the clinic into long-term crisis counseling.

Nor would Jesus have any trouble being executed today, since the Romans were positively queasy about the death penalty compared to the American public. True, few states offer crucifixion facilities, but those who have witnessed them say that electrocutions provide an even grislier end. Future generations of Christians, should there be any, will wear tiny electric chairs around their necks, or kneel down before giant syringes.

The only real problem would be resurrection, which no one has accomplished since Richard Nixon abandoned his life as a thug and returned to this planet as a statesman. Digging up fresh graves, either to get into them or out of them, is regarded these days as vandalism. So R.I.P., Jesus—we can pig out on chocolate bunnies tomorrow, without worrying about being asked to share them.

[1994]

CLASH

OF THE

TITANS

The Warrior Culture

In what we like to think of as "primitive" warrior cultures, the passage to manhood requires the blooding of a spear, the taking of a scalp or head. Among the Masai of eastern Africa and dozens of other human cultures, a man could not marry until he had demonstrated his capacity to kill in battle. Leadership, too, in a warrior society is typically contingent on military prowess and wrapped in the mystique of death. In the Solomon Islands a chief's importance could be reckoned by the number of skulls posted around his door, and it was the duty of the Aztec kings to nourish the gods with the hearts of human captives.

All warrior peoples have fought for the same high-sounding reasons: honor, glory, or revenge. The nature of their real and perhaps not conscious motivations is a subject of much debate. Some anthropologists postulate a murderous instinct, almost unique among living species, in human males. Others discern a materialistic motive behind every fray: a need for slaves, grazing land, or even human flesh to eat. Still others point to the similarities between war and other male pastimes—the hunt and outdoor sports—and suggest that it is boredom, ultimately, that stirs men to fight.

But in a warrior culture it hardly matters which motive is most basic. Aggressive behavior is rewarded whether or not it is innate to the human psyche. Shortages of resources are habitually taken as occasions for armed offensives, rather than for hard thought and innovation. And war, to a warrior people, is of course the highest adventure, the surest antidote to malaise, the endlessly repeated theme of legend, song, religious myth, and personal quest for meaning. It is how men die and what they find to live for.

"You must understand that Americans are a warrior nation," Senator Daniel Patrick Moynihan told a group of Arab leaders in 1990. He said this proudly, and he may, without thinking through the ugly implications, have told the truth. In many ways, in outlook and behavior the United States has begun to act like a primitive warrior culture.

We seem to believe that leadership is expressed, in no small part, by a willingness to cause the deaths of others. After the U.S. invasion of Panama, President Bush exulted that no one could call him "timid"; he was at last a "macho man." The press, in even more primal language, hailed him for succeeding in an "initiation rite" by demonstrating his "willingness to shed blood."

For lesser offices, too, we apply the standards of a warrior culture. Female candidates are routinely advised to overcome the handicap of their gender by talking "tough." Thus, for example, Dianne Feinstein embraced capital punishment, while Colorado senatorial candidate Josie Heath found it necessary to announce that although she is the mother of an eighteen-year-old son, she is prepared to vote for war. Male candidates are finding their military records under scrutiny. No one expects them, as elected officials in a civilian government, to pick up a spear or a sling and fight. But they must state, at least, their willingness to have another human killed.

More tellingly, we are unnerved by peace and seem to find

it boring. When the cold war ended, we found no reason to celebrate. Instead we heated up the "war on drugs." What should have been a public-health campaign, focused on the persistent shame of poverty, became a new occasion for martial rhetoric and muscle flexing. Months later, when the Berlin Wall fell and Communism collapsed throughout Europe, we Americans did not dance in the streets. What we did, according to the networks, was change the channel to avoid the news. Nonviolent revolutions do not uplift us, and the loss of mortal enemies only seems to leave us empty and bereft.

Our collective fantasies center on mayhem, cruelty, and violent death. Loving images of the human body—especially of bodies seeking pleasure or expressing love—inspire us with the urge to censor. Our preference is for warrior themes: the lone fighting man, bandoliers across his naked chest, mowing down lesser men in gusts of automatic-weapon fire. Only a real war seems to revive our interest in real events. With the Iraqi crisis, the networks report, ratings for news shows rose again—even higher than they were for Panama.

And as in any primitive warrior culture, our warrior elite takes pride of place. Social crises multiply numbingly—homelessness, illiteracy, epidemic disease—and our leaders tell us solemnly that nothing can be done. There is no money. We are poor, not rich, a debtor nation. Meanwhile, nearly a third of the federal budget flows, even in moments of peace, to the warriors and their weaponmakers. When those priorities are questioned, some new "crisis" dutifully arises to serve as another occasion for armed and often unilateral intervention.

With Operation Desert Shield, our leaders were reduced to begging foreign powers for the means to support our warrior class. It does not seem to occur to us that the other great northern powers—Japan, Germany, the Soviet Union—might not have found the stakes so high or the crisis quite so threatening. It has not penetrated our imagination that in a world where the powerful, industrialized nation-states are at last at peace, there might be other ways to face down a pint-size third-world warrior state than with massive force of arms. Nor have we begun to see what an anachronism we are in danger of becoming: a warrior nation in a world that pines for peace, a high-tech state with the values of a warrior band.

A leftist might blame "imperialism"; a right-winger would call our problem "internationalism." But an anthropologist, taking the long view, might say this is just what warriors do. Intoxicated by their own drumbeats and war songs, fascinated by the glint of steel and the prospect of blood, they will go forth, time and again, to war.

[1990]

Who's on Main Street?

It was the year that the Democrats were supposed to be dead in the sand, plowed under with Iraq's Republican Guard. None of the big hitters—Mario Cuomo, Jesse Jackson, Al Gore—were willing to run. With George Bush's postwar approval rating at 91 percent, it seemed superfluous to have an election at all, a waste of good media time. Word was that if you had questioned the Persian Gulf war—if you even *looked* like someone who had—you'd never eat lunch in this country again.

Then there was the general, nationwide sense that politics has become an enterprise so loathsome and degrading as to be beneath the attention of a genuine American citizen—politics-as-we-know-it, that is. I was present at the September 1991 meeting where the National Organization for Women's Commission for Responsive Democracy voted to launch a third party, and the tone was of a speak-bitterness session, circa 1970, with the leadership of the Democratic party as a stand-in for the male sex. Someone whispered to me that Ellie Smeal might run for president herself, wrapped in the new NOW party. But by January, it was clear that, except for a coy foray by

Ralph Nader and media-invisible campaigns by Ron Daniels and Larry Agran, the left was going to sit on its hands.

Still, despite all the warnings, candidates came trooping forth—brave men, foolish men, and some who, like Bob Kerrey, seemed to step out onto the stage of history for a moment, scratch their heads, and retreat back into the shelter of their little-known states. One of the potential theme songs rejected by the Bill Clinton campaign was entitled "Any Little Boy Can Be President," and, indeed, at the beginning of primary season we were looking at a Democratic lineup that offered testimony, above all, to the boundless self-esteem of the white male race. As one might expect from these unpromising demographics, silliness abounded from the start. I would try to talk to friends about the primaries and they would look away, embarrassed for me, as if I had brought up the subject of earwax. I would watch for hours—interviews of candidates, interviews with wives and mistresses of candidates, interviews on the ethics of the interviews with the wives and mistresses —and come to in an irritable daze, asking myself: Wait a minute, what was the question?

Because there is always a question. No matter how trivial and degraded the epiphenomena that flit before our eyes— the fit of Paul Tsongas's Speedo suit or the logistics of Clinton's trysts—the responsible citizen is required to ponder and deeply reflect. And the question is: Is there anything in the increasingly febrile and sordid business of presidential politics that could somehow, conceivably, someday, be applied to the project of positive, progressive social change?

This is not, of course, the question that pundits and reporters and anchorpersons encourage us to ask. As seen through the media, a campaign is a primitive gladiatorial contest. Here we have five men (or three or two), and the only issue is who will survive. The media metaphors are consistently militaristic: candidates "battle," get "wounded," and creep back for another round in the "duel." The relevant theoretical reference point would seem to be Robert Bly, who has made us aware that our culture lacks satisfactory male-initiation rites—vision quests, ritual scarifications, testings in combat. Hence the political campaign as primordial rite of male passage, the assumption being that anyone who can survive a campaign must, prima facie, have the right stuff.

It was Clinton who most clearly exemplified the gladiatorial theme. Here we had the classic hero as scripted by Joseph Campbell: born a semiorphan, adopted by an abusive stepfather, marked for greatness by contact with the gods in the form of a boyhood handshake from John F. Kennedy. While most of the candidates seemed strikingly unprepared for the campaign—even omitting, in some cases, such old-fashioned requirements as position papers and campaign staffs—Clinton had spent half of his life laying the groundwork: a Rhodes scholarship; a brilliant, mediagenic wife; an obscure state that no one much visits. In the tradition of a tragic hero, though, he had spent the other half of his life laying land mines along the path before him. First it was Gennifer Flowers testifying in the *Star* as to his prowess at oral sex. Then it was the "scandal of the week": a weasely record on the draft, a dubious reference to Cuomo's ethnicity, unsavory links with S and L scoundrels, a state ethics law that curiously excluded the governor's office from scrutiny, the intimate ties between the state government and Hillary's law firm, the whites-only country club, marijuana at Oxford. After a while, the content of the alleged crimes no longer mattered, and the only media-worthy question was the kind a sportscaster might ask: How was he handling the blows? He was a prince on Flowers, the media judged, but a fool on pot—stopping short only of the classic "Gee, they told me it was a Gauloise."

The pundits prissily decried the nastiness of it all—the squalor, the trivia, the scrapping. Yet they all simultaneously hewed to the belief that there can be no better way to select a leader than through the campaign as trial-by-ordeal. Leading non-candidate Cuomo came closest to articulating this primitive faith in the virtues of combat when he announced, just before the New York primary, that it wouldn't be fair for him to be nominated in a brokered convention, because he hadn't been "tested by the process."

For months, the line of reasoning eluded me. Much as I studied it, I could find no larger relevance in the "process." How could a postmodern campaign—which is chiefly an exercise in fund-raising and deniable mendacity—be regarded as an appropriate test of one's ability to govern a nation? How could an experience that combines elements of fraternity hazing and sleep-deprivation experimentation be a useful prelude to global command?

Then I read something in late March that chilled me to the bone and set my teeth to rattling, as in one of those late-night moments when you catch a glimpse of the terrible emptiness at the heart of it all. What I read was that President Bush was not planning to attend the environmental Earth Summit in Rio de Janeiro, because, in his own words, he was busy "running for the presidency." But he *is* president, I thought, in my innocence. Then it dawned on me: Today, *being* president is really no different from *running* for president. It's about approval ratings and photo ops and damage control and deniability. It's not about running something, it's just about running.

So there was among the electorate a sense of nihilism that went beyond the inadequacies of the choices before us. I heard a radio commentator offer the analysis that we weren't having an election, we were having a "tantrum." People voted to send "messages," particularly on the Republican side, where those who didn't have a dead rodent to lob onto the White House steps were choosing, instead, to mock the very idea of democracy by voting for near-fascist Pat Buchanan. Or people voted for men who were no longer running, like Tsongas in New York. Or they defiantly refused to "rally," withholding state after state from Clinton, the front-runner and media favorite. And however they voted, people seemed to be having bad experiences behind the drawn curtains of the voting booth; they came out telling pollsters they wished they had voted for someone else—though no one could think of whom.

Mostly, though, people didn't bother to vote. Everywhere but New Hampshire, voter turnout fell sharply when compared with 1988. A December 1991 Time/CNN and Yankelovich Clancy Shulman poll found only 23 percent of the citizenry convinced that it made a "big difference" who won the presidential election, 49 percent who believed it made "some difference," and another 23 percent who could discern no difference at all. Even activists I know who four years ago were ringing doorbells for Jesse Jackson had the vague, evasive manner of the man-on-the-street when the microphone is thrust in his face: Well, yes, I suppose it does matter . . . There is, uh, the Supreme Court.

Maybe we are all finally glimpsing that emptiness at the center of things and beginning to conclude that the electoral process, busy and colorful as it may be, no longer has any tangible *product*. This is not, after all, a society in which government impinges on our lives in a kindly and reassuring fashion. We have no national health-care system, no network of government-financed child-care centers, no federal guarantees of higher education. If you are too young for Social Security and Medicare, too wealthy for food stamps and welfare, "federal government" is a remote and abstract concept, manifesting itself chiefly through the post office and the ineluctable IRS.

Once, of course, the federal government was a more significant player on the American scene, and words like "policy" and "programs" meant something even to ordinary people, of the kind who do not reside in think tanks. In a spasm of activism, we got Medicare, Medicaid, Title VII, Title IX, OEO, OSHA . . .

But from the presidential point of view, much of this activity turned out to be unnecessary and distracting from the larger business of getting back into office again. Ronald Reagan was the great simplifier of the executive role—chopping, privatizing, deregulating, and generally abandoning any function of government that might get in the way of the afternoon photo op and the daily tending of polls. As Reagan understood so well, a president must spend his first term running for reelection and his second vying for a slot on Mount Rushmore and a lovely marble library for any papers he may have forgotten to shred. Naturally, a busy president will resent being forced, for example, to waste time chatting with foreigners about the fate of the earth.

Thus we went overnight from a mildly activist government to a mewling, wimpy government: The space program became a galactic embarrassment, serving chiefly to clutter the stratosphere with metallic debris that will prevent any eventual egress from earth. The regulatory agencies nodded out, leaving us with salmonella-ridden eggs, psychoactive sleeping pills, and polyurethane implants in our chests. What infrastructure we have is kept around chiefly out of archaeological interest. Children, long since abandoned by our Scrooge-like welfare state, are now the new pauper class.

The whole notion of government—above the level of school boards and zoning ordinances—has become hypothetical, difficult for the average citizen to verify with his or her sensory equipment. Oh, we know it's there, but the evidence increasingly comes from our television sets; the gulf war, the State of the Union address (with a buildup almost matching the war's), and *Crossfire* every night after dinner. It is government-as-spectacle, and much of it has been a sorry spectacle indeed: a peevish president battling a financially derelict Congress, a white male Senate tormenting a petite black woman, a Supreme Court that you would not leave your young daughter alone with.

Even insiders are beginning to acknowledge that the core of our nation, our common endeavor, is hollow. In March 1992, Senator Warren Rudman, best known for fighting Big Government, announced his forthcoming departure, citing the understandable need to keep busy. In Congress, no fewer than forty-seven incumbents are quitting and going in search of meaningful work. At the end of March, an anonymous Reagan-Bush man, a mid-level Republican federal employee, wrote a chilling op-ed piece in *The New York Times*, revealing that the government "is no longer responsible for anything. The unequivocal message throughout the Federal bureaucracy is that nothing is to be accomplished by this Government except the creation of good feelings and the illusion of action."

Ah, what a ghastly *fin* to the *siècle*! A hundred years ago, only poets spoke of morbidity and dread. The newspaper-reading public believed in Progress, Technology, Good Government—even the bright promise of Socialism. The human mind would stamp its will upon the earth and make it flower, raise up great cities, and succor the hungry and the poor. But "progress" has been revealed to mean deforestation; technology is the oleaginous scum on our ponds, and government an incubus that sucks our wealth and succors almost no one except those who need help least. What we have lost goes beyond mere politics. What we have lost is any faith in our collective intentions—that we can decide something rationally, together, and proceed to get it done. The hand reaches for the lever in the voting booth. The hand falters. The eyes glaze over. The mind wanders. *What* was the question?

Oh well . . . Ah yes, the question . . .

The most obvious lesson of the 1992 primaries is that one need not have the stature of a Lincoln or a Roosevelt to consider a run for the presidency. Prior to the campaign, Clinton was best known for giving a speech at the 1988 Democratic Convention that bored the nation to petulant tears, and Kerrey for his affair with Debra Winger. If these men can do it, anyone can.

It helps, of course, to have held some high-profile public office or at least a key talk-show position. The problem is finding a public office that will not become a blot on one's résumé, since one effect of the Republicans' government-bashing has been to discredit most forms of public service and hence most avenues to the presidency. The House of Representatives, for example, is now widely regarded as a halfway house for long-term miscreants, and governors have the unenviable problem of coming from *states*: after a decade of federal cutbacks affecting everything from health care to highway construction, there is simply no state that one would want to be from.

But if anyone can be president, it must be because the office just isn't worth much anymore. For twelve years, the Republicans gutted the domestic side of government, leaving less and less to administer. Even wars of intervention—the one clear and visible "product" of federal government—need have little impact on American lives and are increasingly waged as spectacles, media events in which "victory" is measured by poll ratings. If large numbers of people were once alienated by Big Government, today they are no less alienated by nongovernment. Nongovernment sat out the recession and the disruption of millions of lives through layoffs and foreclosures. Nongovernment has remained serene in the face of AIDS and our chronic health-care crisis. Nongovernment has been unable to educate children or guarantee the safety of our food and drugs. Without government, what is left then of politics but bluster and manipulation?

A campaign, no matter how honest and progressive, cannot easily undo the damage, which cuts deep into the individual psyche. For years, the Republicans have not only ravaged government, they have mocked it. Again and again we have been told, usually by men who are on the federal payroll, that government can do nothing right, at least nothing that can be accomplished without recourse to firearms. You wouldn't want the post office providing your health care, they tell us. You wouldn't want Big Government taking care of little Kimberly and Sean. Nothing can be done, nothing at all. Poverty is a character flaw. Pollution is growth. Unemployment is destiny. Worse still, anything that government attempts is bound to blow up in our faces, they tell us, offering the War on Poverty as an illustration—an effort said to have coddled the unfortunate so bountifully that they became an army of muggers and layabouts.

Think of the post-Enlightenment despair contained in this hegemonic, conservative conventional wisdom. Think of the even more profound moral surrender implied by our ideological embrace of the unfettered market. There's no point in planning or thinking ahead, we are told in effect—just hang in there and pray for a change in the weather.

We are losing our faith in human agency, in the ability of people, through legal and democratic process, to make their mark on the world. Even a vibrant, bustling campaign will not cure this, because a campaign, by its nature, sucks public attention toward one central point, one limited individual person. What we need, as we all know, is "empowerment," or the strongly held conviction that ordinary people, working together, can actually get something done. And for this, we need, above all, to score a few wins: some strikes that hold fast, with communities organized so that no traitor tries to cross the line; neighbors banding together to fight off foreclosures; women setting up illegal abortion clinics, if necessary, and running them safely and smoothly; students resisting indoctrination into a cruel and hierarchical social order.

A good president, a better president—maybe even any Democrat—could shift the balance of power just enough to inspire more collective defiance from the bottom. The nascent class-consciousness of the middle-class electorate suggests that, if anyone had been prepared and thinking ahead, we *could* have done better in 1992. And there is always 1996.

But the other great lesson of the last calendar year is: You never know. What began in a frenzy of jingoism ended in bitterness and economic collapse. Today's defeat may be tomorrow's opportunity, and opportunities evaporate even as they come into view. There is a wild churning force at work in our media-driven culture, driving us from "crisis" to "crisis," from one mad, collective mood swing on to the next. Those who would win must learn how to ride along with this force, disdaining defeat, grasping every favorable current and eddy, trying and trying, getting the joke. There will be a next time, and this we know for sure: next time is bound to be different.

[1992]

Gulf War II

Early reports from the battlefield were gratifyingly upbeat. Polls taken a mere twenty minutes after George Bush's last-minute bombing of Baghdad showed 83 percent of the public rejoicing in the prospect of a gulf war rerun to coincide with the Superbowl play-offs and the week-long Clinton inauguration. Few in fact could distinguish between the joyous footage of fireworks over Washington and the dazzling views of Baghdad under bombardment. Even Bill Clinton hastened to retract his near-treasonous "I am not obsessed by Saddam" statement and explain that he is indeed obsessed, as is required of a man who has just doffed his jogging gear for the ominous dark pinstripes of high public office.

Of course there are always a few nagging doubts, deliberately encouraged by the naysayers, pacifists, and secret Baath party members among us. Everyone knows, for example, that Barbara and George have been rushing around the White House, taking the batteries out of the smoke alarms, flushing huge wads of incriminating Iran-contra notes down into the plumbing, and otherwise creating a mess that the Clintons will spend weeks cleaning up. It is possible, though few dare say it out loud, that the new little war is more of the same—like the patches of poop left behind on the carpets by first dog Millie.

Then there was Defense Secretary Dick Cheney's unsettling remark that the United States had destroyed all of Iraq's nuclear facilities the first time around. Doesn't he know there had to be a few of them left, otherwise there'd be nothing for us to attack? Perhaps the generals don't tell him everything, since he's only a civilian and won't have any real clout until he finds a new job lobbying for Boeing.

Some even wondered why the United States was bent on obliterating a structure that had only recently been gone over by United Nations inspectors, who had reported that it strongly resembled a machine-tools plant—rather than, say, an assembly line turning out thousands of H-bombs per minute. But who in postindustrial America knows for sure exactly what a "machine tool" is? Better to smash them now, these devilish machine tools, before they can be loaded into missile launchers and hurled at Missoula or Boston.

And even the staunchest patriots were briefly discomfited by the sight of the receptionist at the Hotel Rashid, where the foreign press resides, lying dead on the floor after Sunday's raid. Perhaps this was meant to tie in with the violence-against-women theme that we have come to associate with football weekends, when wife battering reaches its annual highs. Plus there are occasional mutterings about why Iraq gets pounded every time Saddam sneezes, while Serbia calmly continues its program of genocide, undeterred by the loud background sound of "tsk tsk."

But there is no reason not to enjoy Gulf War II every bit as much as the first one. For one thing, bear in mind that no one is killed in these ventures unless Saddam needs a few phony "victims" for his public-relations efforts. Recall those four hundred Iraqi women and children who were fiendishly crammed into a bomb shelter—directly under the bombs! In the vexing case of the hotel receptionist, we have Marlin Fitzwater's personal assurance that American missiles never strike unarmed women, unless they are rabid feminists and followers of Hillary Clinton. The poor receptionist must have been hit by a Scud missile that had been left in the lobby in somebody's suitcase.

In addition, this columnist has gained access to secret Pentagon intelligence (if you will forgive the well-worn oxymoron) showing that the receptionist was not just your average Baathist bimbo with a business degree. No, she was in fact a nuclear physicist who had been using the hotel credit-card imprint machine to make fissionable plutonium pellets—right under the eyes of the Western press!

So relax and enjoy Bush's last little war with a clear conscience and unfurrowed brow. There won't be another one for a couple of months, when Clinton will no doubt be pressured to prove that, despite Hillary and his draft problems and all, he's as big a man as George.

[1993]

Somalia—

the Ratings War

Somalia, let's face it, has been a big disappointment. There've been no yellow ribbons or rallies in support of the troops. Go into a bar and no one will offer to whip you for questioning the necessity of armed intervention. In fact, no one much mentions Somalia at all, least of all at dinner parties or in the supermarket checkout line.

We expect more from our annual holiday-season interventions. It is said, after all, that the entire program was initiated by the profamily movement, with the idea that the American family could not survive the ghastly togetherness imposed by Christmas without something more riveting than football to watch.

First we had Panama, and what a thrill it was! Never mind that hundreds, perhaps thousands, of Panamanians inadvertently died in the process, or that the cocaine traffic actually increased after Manuel Noriega had been dispatched to Miami. It was breathtaking, the way we moved into a nation as if it were one of our own local crack houses and arrested the head of state. If we could do it to one, why not do it to others? There were hopes that future Christmases would bring us footage of François Mitterrand being pursued by Marines through the back alleys of Paris, or Margaret Thatcher dodging the infantry in the shrubs of Hyde Park.

Then there was Iraq, the first made-for-TV war, offering weeks of wholesome family viewing. All right, it wasn't much of a war, since the enemy refused to participate, but it was stirring to see thousands of Americans camping out in the desert for months without even a beer.

Naturally we expected the Somalia operation, tailored as it was for Christmas consumption, to be the best midwinter intervention yet. At first everyone was titillated by the novelty of using troops—not to pulverize little children in their bomb shelters but to succor and save. Imagine, the press crowed, a warm cuddly intervention that even a pacifist has to love! Plus there are the obvious opportunities for white racial chauvinism. Give 'em a country, our newsmen seem to be saying night after night, and they turn it into a ghetto: Drugs, gangs, armed teenagers ruling the streets! Not a tidbit of infrastructure that hasn't been vandalized and sold for scrap!

So why, instead of filling us with righteous jingoistic pride, does Somalia evoke this creepy sense of unease? The answer, a psychotherapist might say, is that Americans are, as usual, "in denial," and that the repressed has a nasty habit of raising its head. There is a reason why every Somalian boy has a weapon that weighs more than he does, and the reason, we vaguely recall, can be traced back to us: on the basis of strategic considerations that have long since been forgotten, the United States, along with the USSR, armed these people and fomented the civil war that preempted food production and all other activities of daily life. But it would be depressing to admit that in Somalia, as in Panama and Iraq, we are simply cleaning up a mess of our own devising.

There's another possible reason why Somalia isn't fun, something so embarrassing that I hesitate to put it in print: deep down, we envy the Somalians. Yes, we see their frail bodies, flapping in the hot African wind, but then the commercial comes on—for Metrecal, or Nutri/System, or calorie-free aerobic-style chocolate—and secretly we wonder: How do they do it? And if they can do it so effortlessly over there, why are we still running on treadmills and dining on celery for lunch?

I'm all for intervention, mind you. I'm just not sure we're going about it right. When the Somalians were merely another hungry third-world people, we sent them guns. Now that they are falling down dead from starvation, we send them troops. Some may see in this a tidy metaphor for the entire relationship between north and south. But it would make a whole lot more sense nutritionally—as well as providing infinitely more vivid viewing—if the Somalians could be persuaded to eat the troops.

[1993]

Battlin' Bill's

Initiation Rite

One doesn't have to be an admirer of mass rape to experience a sick, sinking feeling at the prospect of U.S. intervention in Bosnia. Well, perhaps one does feel a sneaky bit of respect for the Serbs, who have managed to take the somewhat forbidding institution of genocide and de-industrialize it, bringing it down to human scale and potentially within reach of every neighborhood council and block committee. For what man has not, at some point, gazed upon his neighbor's house or car or wife, and thought, Jeez, a couple of rounds of automatic fire, and all that could be mine, with the power saw thrown in!

The drumbeats have been sounding for months. In *The New York Times*, Leslie Gelb warned Bill Clinton that "without successes, he will lack the power to lead," and as examples of "successes," he offered Ronald Reagan's dazzling conquest of Grenada and George Bush's "crusade" in Iraq. And it's true; here we are 5,000 days into the Clinton administration—or is it only 100?—and no one has died in the heat of battle, at least not outside of Waco, Texas. The beast stirs. Normally mild-mannered columnists strip to the waist, pound their gray-haired chests, and raise the cry for blood.

The word "primitive" would seem to apply. One's mind drifts inevitably to the Sepik River tribes of New Guinea, the Jivaro of South America, and the many other cultures who used to make successful head-hunting a prerequisite for the privileges of manhood. Among certain Gallic tribes in the pre-Roman days, a boy did not become a man until he had killed in battle. Closer to our own time and place, there was the veritable bar mitzvah that accompanied George Bush's invasion of Panama.

Then there is the obvious problem of the public attention span. For months now, we have heard of nothing but "deficit reduction" and "stimulus packages" and "managed competition." We struggle to pay attention, but the only ill likely to be cured by, say, Clinton's health-reform proposals is long-term, drug-resistant insomnia. Fondly, we recall the assurances that Bush would "have an interest in governing." He never did, bless his poll-driven little heart, focusing instead on the more colorful issues of flag burning and Saddam Hussein.

So why do I still hang back, tormented by doubts, from the crowd demanding intervention in Bosnia? The reason, of course, is Waco. Americans are not known for their restraint in matters involving armed confrontation. There is a tendency, in fact, to flip into a state of uncontrollable, wolfish rage—*lyssa* was the ancient Greek word for it—whenever the slightest opportunity arises for the exercise of lethal force. A uniformed American with firepower is much like a three-year-old with a garden hose: someone in whose presence no one can expect to remain dry and composed for long.

For days now, television has been juxtaposing blackened bodies exhumed from Waco with those uncovered in Bosnian basements—without anybody making the obvious and ominous connection. Janet Reno came forth, exhibiting the emotions appropriate to someone who has just held a cigarette lighter to a kerosene-soaked child—dismay, that is, and a touchingly poignant regret. The children had to be saved, she explained, they were in danger of being abused. And no doubt a staff of psychiatric experts had determined that the conditions of the siege, including constant high-volume bombardment with Nancy Sinatra songs, was no longer optimal for the serene exercise of parenting skills. So the children were indeed saved, though in the military, not the biblical, sense.

How long, then, before we are forced to watch Madeleine Albright, or some other grandmotherly addition to the Clinton team, explaining that those babies in Belgrade should not have been playing in a tank factory and had been molested by their daddies anyway?

Rodney King is another example of the American tendency to use a SWAT team where, in any normal human community, a single unarmed constable might do. All right, King was driving too fast and could easily have hurt himself. Plus there is the law of police science which holds that any black man who exceeds the recommended shuffling pace is a perpetrator pure and simple, unless he is doing so in the service of sport. Even so, one jury out of two found two out of four of King's torturers guilty. And all of us, from time to time, are saddened to learn of some elderly couple's home ransacked, furniture splintered and flower beds torn up, in the course of a routine drug bust that happened to have the wrong address.

Armed overkill has become the rule. Think of Panama, where hundreds—thousands?—were killed in the process of a single arrest. Or Iraq, where hundreds of thousands were incinerated to "send a message" to Saddam Hussein. If the latest peace plan breaks down, what will it take to convey to the Serbs the emerging Euro-American consensus that genocide is, generally speaking, frowned upon? Air strikes are all that have been suggested, but recent experience shows that even the smartest bombs have trouble telling the difference between a day-care center and a nuclear-weapons facility. And no one has yet invented the Rhodes-scholar bomb that will pass over all the sweet-faced Serbian antiwar activists and get only the nasty Chetnik rapists.

Hence my concern that any intervention be as multilateral as possible, even if millions of troops are required. There will need to be at least one Dane or Swiss for every American soldier, just to keep an eye out for the signs of incipient overkill: little flecks of foam about the mouth, for instance, or a reddish glow to the eyes. Not that Americans are a mean and blood-thirsty race. It's just that we share a deep belief—from Janet Reno to, apparently, David Koresh, from Vietnam to Panama—that burnt offerings are just as appealing to the Christian god as they were to Zeus before him.

[1994]

Willy/Woody

It cannot be a coincidence that Woody Allen lost his custody case in the same week that a secret military coup installed David Gergen in the White House. Here we have two men —Bill Clinton and Allen—differing markedly in height, weight, ethnic background, and known sexual predilections. Yet both come from the Democratic side of the political spectrum, and both, incredibly enough, got their comeuppance within the space of a few short days. No way this could have happened, the conspiracy-minded are muttering, if Oliver Stone had not been distracted by his *Wild Palms* venture.

In both cases, the tragedy had been building for months, if not years. An early sign of Clinton's approaching downfall was the famed haircut on a Los Angeles runway, with its obvious Samson-like overtones. Then the Secret Service switched from guarding the president to spying on him and running to the press every time Hillary clobbered him with a vase, or perhaps it was a Bible. Soon the entire armed forces were in open revolt. An Air Force general denounced Clinton as "draft-dodging, pot-smoking, womanizing," not to mention flagrantly "gay-loving." At the Memorial Day ceremonies, dozens of Viet vets —apparently so addled by posttraumatic stress syndrome that they confused Clinton with Johnson and Nixon—raucously blamed him for the deaths of their comrades.

So, too, with Woody Allen's tragic descent into incest: you could see it coming from a long way back. I am not referring to the obvious fact, often cited by the vulgar-minded, that his screenplays uniformly center on the relationships of a middle-aged loser with females too young to vote. No, I am referring to the mounting claustrophobia of his oeuvre, concerned as it was with the same small group of neurotic heterosexuals, the same Upper West Side neighborhood.

Many have wondered why Woody couldn't have found a gorgeous, intelligent, postpubescent woman to keep him company when he tired of Mia. But where would he have found her? One of his films was titled *Interiors*, but this could equally well have been the title of them all: his was a sadly under-populated version of New York—devoid of poor people and persons of color, inhabited solely by a half-dozen wealthy white people, along with their physicians and shrinks. No wonder, when he wanted a date, he could think of nowhere to look but the nursery.

At the subconscious level of the zeitgeist, all things are connected, so we should have grasped the link between Clinton and Allen over a year ago. Last summer, for example, news of the Amy Fisher trial bled over into the Democratic National Convention, providing a low, cynical counterpoint to the over-rated Year of the Woman. Then, a few weeks later, news of the Woody–Soon-Yi affair virtually preempted the Republican Convention. They tried to warn us, those intrepid Republicans, that Woody represented the Democrats' sick, twisted version of "family values," that in fact Woody and Willy were one.

Who listened then? It seemed so farfetched. Yet with hindsight we can see the many parallels and strange overlaps between the two cases. There is the obvious matter of their wives, or, in the case of Mia, unwife. Both are blond and saintly: the fragile, hollow-cheeked Mia; Hillary in the *New York Times Magazine* caricature of her as Saint Joan, hands crossed ecstatically over armored chest. Both are driven by preternaturally powerful maternal instincts: Mia with her throngs of multicultural kids; Hillary and her famed obsession with the welfare of low-income children.

And both were betrayed by their men in similar fashion. Mia had no way of knowing she was raising up little Soon-Yi, and possibly Dylan, to star in Daddy's private photo sessions. Nor did she realize that her portrayal, in *Husbands and Wives*, of a self-absorbed hysteric was part of Woody's secret preparation for the custody bid. Similarly, Hillary must have believed she was married to a fine liberal fellow who shared her concern for the tiny orphans and beggars who scamper through our streets. What a shock it must be every time he fulminates against lazy, cheating welfare recipients—who are, for the most part, small children themselves—or when he fecklessly abandons some social or environmental reform that might have given kids of all classes a chance to grow up!

I could point to many other curious connections. There was Woody Allen's film about the infinitely mutable Zelig, who we see now perfectly foreshadows the Clinton presidency as he evolved from check-shirted populist to unapproachable monarch, from mild liberal to Reagan heir. But one thing should already be abundantly clear: the intelligent, sensitive, faux-liberal man, Woody or Will, is not the "new man" we feminists have been clamoring for. He more nearly resembles a viper in the nest. The Gergen coup is regrettable, of course, but at least we will finish out the term without romantic illusions about kindly male saviors to protect and provide for our children.

It is impossible, at this point, to tell how far the convergence between Allen and Clinton will go. But there are rumors that

Woody is tiring of Soon-Yi, who has reached the hoary age of twenty-two, and chances are that the court will bar him from preying on Mia's numerous other little girls. So it will be Woody and Chelsea next—unless, of course, Hillary can band together with Mia and put a stop to this.

[1993]

Jones v. Clinton

By now every schoolchild in America can recite the story. Paula Jones, a former employee of the state of Arkansas, says she was summoned one evening to then-Governor Bill Clinton's hotel room. Expecting perhaps to be consulted on industrial policy, Ms. Jones instead found the governor in an affectionate mood. After venturing a few brief verbal preliminaries, the governor unzipped his fly and—so Ms. Jones alleges—*dropped his pants* right down to his knees.

Possibly the story was invented simply to embarrass the president as he struggled to execute another of his celebrated high-wire Haiti flip-flops. But common sense tells us that no woman could have made this up. In the female fantasy version, there is champagne, some urgent whispering about line-item budgets or the balance of trade with Missouri, perhaps a discreet back rub in the manner of Virginia's Senator Robb. Certainly no self-respecting woman could invent a scenario in which her seducer abruptly lays bare his genitals and offers an exciting come-on along the lines of "Hey babe, wanna test drive this beauty?"

But let the pundits debate the truth of Ms. Jones's accusations. The true patriot should be more concerned, if not fully alarmed, about the president's social and sexual skills. How, for example, did he ever lure Hillary into his vast, french-fry-scented embrace? One pictures young Bill stalking her through the law-school library stacks, then—flash!—leaping out from behind Property or Torts, naked member enticingly out and in hand.

Admittedly, Bill has spent much of his adult life living in mansions, which are a notoriously poor place to meet friendly young women. His approach would have been suaver, one suspects, if he had spent more time in female-rich environments such as tenements, welfare offices, or feminist bookshops. No wonder that, when faced with an empty hotel bed, he could think of no option but to order up a companion through room service.

But, Bill, there is no reason for every romantic encounter to end in press conferences and bizarre tabloid stories. In the interests of national security and certainly dignity, here are a few tips for an upgraded, scandal-free social life:

First, never proceed directly to the genitals, insistent as these organs may be. Surely you are familiar with the notion of "foreplay," and, if not, the surgeon general would gladly fill you in. The purpose of the preliminaries is to give the whole thing a vaguely consensual air and thus diminish the grounds for prosecution. For example, it is smart to have a few topics of common interest to discuss before the time comes for the unzipping of flies. Hillary's 1,300-page health proposal has been known to put many people in the mood for bed. Or you could develop some new interests and conversational themes —foreign policy has often been suggested.

Second, it is unwise to use the constabulary to gather up potential lady-friends. Ms. Jones claims to have been fetched to the governor's boudoir by a state trooper in the course of his duties. This is bad form. Many women respond poorly to uniformed pimps, and prefer, as John F. Kennedy knew, to use the Mafia as a middleman.

Third, don't be so cheap. Even a low-wage clerical worker deserves some refreshments before settling down to fellate an important public official. Take-out from McDonald's will not do if the lady in question is over fifteen, and forget about Hillary's cookies.

In fact, it would probably be wise to dump Hillary, as your advisers have been urging for reasons of their own. Few women relish a hotel-room quickie with the husband of a world-powerful woman—even when he refers to her, as Gennifer Flowers reported in her 1992 *Hustler* interview, as "Hilla the Hun." True, Hillary is bound to fight back in embarrassing ways—by charging some sort of "cruelty" no doubt. But remember that it is you who control the courts, and capital punishment is a snap in Arkansas.

Imagine a Hillary-less future! Whitewater would float away like poultry scum on an Arkansas stream, and fresh candidates for first lady would be beating on your hotel-room doors.

[1994]

Haiti Explained

Countless readers have written to this columnist in the last week begging for some clue as to our mission in Haiti. "Isn't it unusual," many have asked, "for a military force to change sides in the middle of an engagement?" Not at all, according to top-level Pentagon researchers. History offers numerous examples of mid-battle switches of allegiance, not all of them involving sixth-century Visigoths or Croatian irregulars. Even the participants in the so-called "charge" of the Light Brigade were, according to leading revisionist historians, bedeviled by ambivalence and loudly debating whether to side with the Russians or the Turks—even, alas, as their mounts achieved an unstoppable speed. So no one should look askance at the United States for appearing to combat Raoul Cédras, then Aristide, and digging in now against the sinister force that almost wiped us out in Somalia, namely, the dread "mission creep."

"Does the U.S. have one Haitian policy or two, or perhaps some number in between?" is another question readers have raised. Here I must refer you to the delicate matter of "perception," which plays such a commanding role in our system of governance. Clinton, in a rare moment of lucidity and calm, looked at the Haitian junta and saw "rapists" and "thugs." But this has nothing to do with the fact that Jimmy Carter, arriving in Port-au-Prince, found Lieutenant General Cédras cuddling a bevy of street-dwelling orphans while his wife crocheted elegant shrouds for their poor departed parents—victims, like so many others, of an inexplicably "violent culture."

The underlying principle here, which has guided U.S. foreign policy for decades, is that of the attraction of like for like. A cursory glance reveals that our free-lance negotiating team —Jimmy Carter (known to detractors as "Kim's toy" and "plaything of dictators"), Colin "Desert Storm" Powell, and Sam "Beef Up the Military Budget" Nunn—consisted entirely of light-skinned millionaires with a passion for affairs of state. Who, then, were they to pass the time with in Port-au-Prince? Surely not coconut vendors. Similarly, armies tend to favor other armies over shabbily dressed throngs of civilians sporting torture wounds. This is especially true when the armies in question share cherished memories of their alma mater in Fort Benning, Georgia, and of many earnest hours in Interrogation class, not to mention Anti-Communism 101.

"Could there be more to this than meets the eye," some of the craftier readers want to know, "some intra–White House intrigue, perhaps?" Happily, there is no basis to the rumor that the invasion was engineered by Clinton spokeswoman Dee Dee Myers, in order to distract the president while she wrestled Leon Panetta to the ground and gnawed on his earlobe until he agreed to let her keep her post. The other possibility, that the whole thing was a scheme to get Warren Christopher's attention, cannot be discounted, though in this respect it has tragically failed.

"Are there vital American interests at stake?" some have inquired. To which I must say, At last, an intelligent question! Yes, of course, there are always vital American interests at stake: oil in the gulf; those lovely coral earrings, in the case of Grenada; and—though few in the outside world realize it —the U.S. is almost totally dependent on Haiti for its supply of baseballs. This season's so-called baseball strike has, in fact, been a voluntary effort to control consumption, but an alarming dependency remains. All our baseballs are stitched together by Haitian women for wages of five to ten cents an hour, apparently out of sheer love for the game.

Imagine if we had to import our baseballs from, say, Belgium, where labor costs would drive up the price of each ball to $159 or more. Greedy fans would stampede in their efforts to catch fly balls. The sport would be ruined. Hence our Haitian mission as it is emerging at this very moment: to give the Haitian military a refresher course in clean, high-tech methods of crowd control—i.e., labor suppression—before Aristide returns. So naturally there is some confusion about which side we are on: we like our baseballs cheap, but they shouldn't actually be dripping with blood.

[1994]

Tale of a Whale

I went to Key West to escape the persistent delusion that the tape of Rodney King's beating was in fact a bit of censored footage from the ground war in Iraq. Four days into my recovery, and much cheered by Anthony Lewis's admission that he had perhaps mistakenly encouraged the dreadful carnage of Operation Desert Storm, I awoke to a commotion on the beach adjacent to our rented compound. A half-dozen young people were crouching in the water around what appeared to be a huge black fish. Eager to participate in the marine biology lesson, I waded out but was shooed off by a hulking fellow with a button featuring a ferocious eagle affixed to his bandanna—another Desert Storm reference, I could not help but note. It was a beached pilot whale, he told me impatiently, and no one was allowed in the water or even on the beach.

Hours passed while the officious but otherwise admirable rescue team busied itself spraying, shading, and propping up the suicidal whale. I settled in a deck chair to meditate on the psychology that could approve the slaughter of hundreds of thousands of humans and yet rally so nobly to save the life of one poor, stranded mammal. Perhaps I had even misjudged my flag-waving neighbors up north, to whom the entire Persian Gulf venture must have seemed one vast and thoroughly decent rescue mission. The sun was warm, the water turquoise, and the whale's benefactors were pleasingly integrated as to race and sex.

Toward noon, as we all awaited the truck or helicopter that was to fetch the whale to some veterinary haven up the Keys, one of the rescuers screamed, "Shark attack!" This was a bizarre and truly alarming turn of events, considering that the whale and its human companions were in no more than three feet of water, a few yards from dry sand belonging to a luxury hotel. Some of the civilian onlookers later claimed to have seen a black object, and perhaps a fin, moving in the water, but there is no doubt about what happened next. The same muscular fellow who had warned me away earlier took up a stick and began to beat the water furiously. A blood-red stain appeared. When the dead "shark" was hauled out, it was revealed to be a baby pilot whale, which the larger one, perhaps encouraged by so much nurturing attention, had trustingly produced.

While the bereft mother was hoisted into a truck with the sinister label "Seafood," I huddled with my friends to discuss the day's impact on the six-year-old in our company, a lovely child with no prior experience of infanticide. The rescuers' story, it soon emerged, was that the baby whale was premature, stillborn, and, anyway, unbruised. I hope, for the sake of our biped species, that an investigation being conducted by the National Marine Fisheries Service bears that out. In the meantime, I take some comfort from the un–Desert Storm–like finale to the frantic scene in the water: upon seeing the dead baby whale, the man who had beaten the water with a stick, who wore the eagle emblem on his bandanna, ran onto the beach, threw down his stick, collapsed on the sand, pulled his shirt up over his head, and sobbed.

[1991]

Acknowledgments

LIFE IN THE POSTMODERN FAMILY

"Burt, Loni, and Our Way of Life" (*Time*, 1993; revised 1994)

"Want a Child? Take My Son" (*Time*, 1993)

"Cultural Baggage" (*New York Times Magazine*, 1992)

"Housework Is Obsolescent" (*Time*, 1993)

"The Wretched of the Hearth" (*The New Republic*, 1990)

"Sex and the Married Woman" (*Mirabella*, 1992)

"The Economics of Cloning" (*Time*, 1993)

"Fun with Cults" (*The Guardian*, 1994)

"Oh, *Those* Family Values" (*Time*, 1994)

BODY ISSUES

"Why Don't We Like the Human Body?" (*Time*, 1991)

"Stamping Out a Dread Scourge" (*Time*, 1992)

"The Naked Truth about Fitness" (*Lear's*, 1990)

"So's Your Old Lady" (*The Nation*, 1994)

"A New Boom to Die For" (*The Nation* and *The Guardian*, 1993)

"Coming of Age" (*Lear's*, 1993)

SEX SKIRMISHES AND GENDER WARS

"Women Would Have Known" (*Time*, 1991)

"Feminism Confronts Bobbittry" (*Time*, 1994)

"Sorry, Sisters, This Is Not the Revolution" (*Time*, 1990)
"What Do Women Have to Celebrate?" (*Time*, 1992)
"Making Sense of *la différence*" (*Time*, 1992)
"Kiss Me, I'm Gay" (*Time*, 1993)

IN THE REALM OF THE SPECTACLE

"The Decline of the Universe" (*The Guardian*, 1994)
"Prewatched TV" (*The Guardian*, 1994)
"Blood on the Temple Steps" (*The Guardian*, 1992)
"Gone with the Wind" (*The Guardian*, 1993)
"Readers' Block" (*The Nation*, 1993)
"Camelot Redux" (*Lear's*, 1993)
"Star Power" (*The Guardian*, 1993)
"Won't Somebody Do Something Silly?" (*Time*, 1993)
"The Blight of the Living Dead" (*The Guardian*, 1993)
"Paying Attention to O.J." (*The Guardian*, 1994)
"The Triumph of Trash" (unpublished, 1994)

THE SNARLING CITIZEN

"Teach Diversity—with a Smile" (*Time*, 1991)
"Down to the Fundamentals" (*The Guardian*, 1992)
"Why the Religious Right Is Wrong" (*Time*, 1992)
"Maintaining the Crime Supply" (*The Guardian*, 1994)
"Why Do They Keep Coming?" (*The Guardian*, 1993)
"Tired and Out of Compassion" (*The Guardian*, 1993)
"We're Number One!" (*The Guardian*, 1994)
"Onward, Christian Lite!" (*Time*, 1994)
"Kicking the Big One" (*Time*, 1994)

TRAMPLING ON THE DOWN-AND-OUT

"Welfare: A White Secret" (*Time*, 1991)
"S-M as Public Policy" (*The Guardian*, 1993)
"How Labor's Love Was Lost" (*The Guardian*, 1993)
"An Epidemic of Munchausen's Syndrome" (*The Guardian*, 1993)
"Real Babies, Illegitimate Debates" (*Time*, 1994)

"Honor to the Working Stiffs" (*Time*, 1991)
"Fear of Easter" (*The Guardian*, 1994)

CLASH OF THE TITANS

"The Warrior Culture" (*Time*, 1990)
"Who's on Main Street?" (*Mother Jones*, 1992)
"Gulf War II" (*The Guardian*, 1993)
"Somalia—the Ratings War" (*The Guardian*, 1993)
"Battlin' Bill's Initiation Rite" (*The Nation*, 1994)
"Willy/Woody" (*The Nation*, 1993)
"Jones v. Clinton" (*The Guardian*, 1994)
"Haiti Explained" (*The Guardian*, 1994)
"Tale of a Whale" (*The Nation*, 1991)